# Hunting
# Whitetails
# Successfully

# Hunting Whitetails Successfully

## Hunter's Information Series®
## North American Hunting Club
### Minneapolis, Minnesota

*Hunting Whitetails Successfully*

Library of Congress Catalog Card Number 84-061177
ISBN 0-914697-05-6

Printed in U.S.A.

23

# Contents

# Dedication

*"To Sherry, my favorite hunting companion."*

**J. Wayne Fears**

# Acknowledgments

This fine book is truly a volume which will benefit beginning and veteran whitetail hunters alike. Its success is due to the hunting experience and writing talent of the author, but his efforts are supported by a dedicated, behind-the-scenes staff.

Thanks to Senior Vice President Mark LaBarbera, Writer/Editor Chuck Weschler, noted whitetail biologist Pat Karns, Editor Bill Miller, Associate Editor Steve Pennaz, Vice President of Product Marketing Mike Vail and Marketing Manager Linda Kalinowski.

Almost all of the photographs for this book were taken by the author, J. Wayne Fears. The remainder were provided by the author's wife, Sherry; sons, Chris and Jeff, and by Mark LaBarbera.

**Steven F. Burke, President**
**North American Hunting Club**

# Foreword

I have a mythical assignment to explore and hunt white-tailed deer in one of America's vast regions of roadless wilderness. The stipulations are that I go afoot and carry all my gear and provisions in a backpack with the expectation of living out of my packsack for several weeks. I am allowed one guide or one companion to help me fulfill the mission.

The gentleman I choose to accompany me must have a number of specialized qualifications. He must be an expert deer hunter and rugged enough to take almost any hardship, yet experienced and wise enough to avoid them. He must know what necessities we should include to keep our pack load to a minimum. He must know trails and how to get through country without them. He must be steeped in the basics of camping in comfort and safety. He must have knowledge of wild foods, which surely will be needed to supplement our store-bought supplies, and perhaps even to survive. One of his strong points has to be a knowledge of photography, for that is part of our assignment. Cheerfulness and sharing are most important assets.

Chances are, I could find a number of friends and acquaintances who might excel in one or another of the above categories, but my list of those who blanket all of these qualifications is very limited indeed.

Among those few is J. Wayne Fears, author of many articles

in national magazines and a number of books on camping, fishing, hunting, canoeing, and back-country cooking. I told him once that he and I would make a great team because he liked to cook and I liked to eat.

Now Wayne has come up with a new book—this one on deer hunting. As in all his writings, it is not only well-written and enjoyable reading; it is detailed, thorough and precise, and it covers white-tailed deer from fawn to feast.

Chapter by chapter he takes you through all the stages, with sound advice for the beginning hunter, and suggestions and tricks the oldest trophy hunter will find valuable. He gets into the personalities of bucks and does, and shows how you can use this knowledge to your advantage. You will find information on the feeding habits of deer, so you will know where and when to look; the expedience of pre-season and in-season scouting for rubs, scrapes, and other sign; how to attract reluctant bucks; where to place your chunk of lead or broadhead for a clean kill; how to treat your prize from trophy to chops. As far as my knowledge goes, he leaves out no detail for a successful and enjoyable hunt.

A word or two more about J. Wayne Fears. From his toddling days, his world has been the outdoors. It is rumored that he could identify a fish hook before he recognized a nipple— something he may or may not be able to verify. As a youngster, he spent all of his spare hours in the outdoors and, by way of the Army, went from high school into Auburn University where he graduated in wildlife management. He continued his studies through a Master's Degree at the University of Georgia and from there went into the wildlife management consulting and big game hunting business.

Over the years he helped to establish sound game programs on the lands of corporations, estates, and individuals. Possibly his greatest wildlife management job was with a major paper company in western Alabama, where his white-tailed deer management program was recognized as one of the nation's best. The success ratio among his hunters was exceptionally high.

He remained with the paper company for over seven years before leaving to devote full time to freelance writing and eventually to creating his own chain of high-quality hunting lodges, Alabama Backcountry Lodges, Inc., with expansive tracts of land and an abundance of game.

Through it all, Wayne polished his expertise in deer hunting, camping, canoeing, wilderness survival, and other outdoor skills. He has two basic loves—the outdoors and writing. With the excellent way he presents his experience and knowledge, he has developed markets for his stories throughout the outdoor field. You must look hard for an outdoor magazine that does not carry his byline.

I know of no one more qualified to bring a lifetime of hunting experience, as well as the charm of deer and deer hunting, to a book like this. After you read it, you will re-read it and heartily agree.

*Charlie Elliott*

4

*Hunter checks the chewed-up branch above a whitetail's scrape.*

# 1

# Getting to Know Whitetails

The white-tailed deer ranks as one of the smartest and most elusive game animals in the world. No hunter can match the whitetail's stealth or its uncanny ability to detect and avoid danger. For this reason, the hunter must do everything he can to shift the odds in his favor. And, the best way of doing that is to familiarize himself with deer behavior and habitat preferences. Without this knowledge, the hunter is not hunting; he is simply walking through the woods, depending on luck to be successful.

### Senses of Deer

As any experienced hunter knows, the whitetail's senses of hearing, sight, and smell are amazingly keen. The deer's large ears act as radar and are always tuned in for any out-of-the-ordinary sound. A loud step in the leaves, the snap of a twig, branches scraping against a nylon jacket, or a loose swivel on a rifle—all will put a buck on the alert. Deer also listen to woodland creatures—the chatter of a squirrel, the alarm call of a crow, or the scream of a bluejay that reveals the hunter's presence.

In addition to their radar-like hearing, deer can spot the slightest movement. Because of the whitetail's extraordinary sense of sight, many hunters wear various types of camouflage clothing to blend in with the background. Also, hunters learn to move slowly and to avoid any quick, attention-getting movements, such as swinging their arms.

For many years, biologists believed that deer were color blind. Early work on the structure of the whitetail's retina did not reveal any color-sensing, or *cone*, cells. But recently, researchers using electron microscopes have found cone cells in the eyes of whitetails. The cells, however, are few and far between compared to those found in other species with good color perception. Further research by Michigan State University and the Michigan Department of Natural Resources has demonstrated that deer can detect the color red and its various shades.

The whitetail's strongest sense is its amazing ability to smell. If you ever watch a deer in the woods, you will see that its nose is constantly working. Hunters should always take into account the wind speed and direction, and other factors that determine how scents are carried through the woods and fields. Throughout this book, I will stress the use of different scents to mask your smell. Before you hunt, think about what you will carry that

*Deer rely on their keen senses of smell, sight, and hearing to detect danger. Curious animals, they sometimes get themselves into trouble by investigating strange smells and sounds.*

might give off an odor foreign to deer. Your cigarettes, gun oil, coffee, food, deodorant and many other items let deer know you are in the woods.

### Deer Sounds

Contrary to what many hunters think, whitetails make several different sounds. Many times you can locate deer by pinpointing their calls. A fawn looking for its mother bleats somewhat like a sheep. A hurt or wounded deer will make a sound like that of a goat. All deer will snort, either when alarmed or to make an unidentified object move. I have, however, observed deer that snort for no apparent reason. The sound is like the expulsion of air under pressure. If hunting during the rut, be alert for the grunting sound of a buck. The sound is similar to the low grunts of a hog.

### Breeding & Reproduction

The breeding season marks the beginning of the whitetail's life cycle. Depending on the latitude, breeding may take place anytime from September to late February.

Hunters and wildlife biologists generally refer to the peak of the rut as that period when, in a given area, most of the breeding activity occurs. However, the actual season in which successful breeding can take place is usually much longer than most hunters believe.

The length of the rut is generally determined by latitude and day length. In the more northern areas of the whitetail range, such as New York and Wisconsin, changes in day length are pronounced. With the shorter days of fall, the rutting activity increases and ends within a relatively short period of time. In the southern states, differences in day length are not as pronounced and the breeding season lasts for several weeks. Whitetails near the Equator actually breed year-round.

Genetics can also play a role in the peak and duration of the rut. In Alabama, where deer from several stocks have been introduced, those originating from Michigan were observed to have different breeding dates than those with North Carolina ancestry. Meanwhile, deer originally imported from Texas displayed yet another breeding period.

Breeding in doe fawns is dependent upon their physical condition. Large doe fawns may breed when only six to nine months old, generally bearing a single fawn. Doe fawns that have not reached physical maturity in their first year will wait until 16 to 19 months old. Weather, growing season, range conditions, and heredity all play a role in the breeding scheme. The number of fawns and yearling does breeding may vary tremendously in the same population from one year to the next, which is important for the wildlife manager and hunter to understand for proper herd management.

The breeding season for the buck begins about the time it sheds its velvet. It's at this time that his male hormone, called *testosterone*, begins to increase and be noticed, signalling physical and behavioral changes that accompany breeding activities.

From the time he sheds his velvet until actual breeding takes place, the buck undergoes a series of changes. As the level of testosterone increases, he becomes less wary and more vulnerable to accidents and hunting. He acts somewhat like a headstrong teenager, making rash judgments and often blundering into trouble that he would normally avoid.

During the rut, the buck actively scent-marks his area to advertise his presence, both to challenge neighboring bucks and to attract does.

The *estrus*, or heat period, in the doe lasts about 24 hours. If not bred, a doe will come into heat again in about 28 days. An unbred doe is capable of five estrus cycles in a single year.

The normal gestation period for white-tailed deer is just under seven months. Generally, does giving birth for the first time have only one fawn. Older does commonly have twins and sometimes triplets.

The first 48 hours are critical to the survival of the newborn fawn. Its chances may be lessened if the mother suffers from poor nutrition during the last two to three months of her pregnancy, which may be the result of a prolonged winter in northern climes or a poor growing season elsewhere. Fawns that survive their first two days of life have a good chance of making it into the deer population the following fall.

At birth, the fawn weighs between four and seven pounds. The first three or four weeks of its life, it stays in one general location, which is determined by the doe. During this period, the doe will come to the fawn so it can nurse. The fawn's spots provide excellent camouflage, allowing it to blend into almost any background. It instinctively lies flat and motionless when danger is near. In addition, it is completely odorless for the first few days of its life. Other than nursing time, the doe stays away from the fawn to keep her odor from giving away its location.

*Fawns are born in secluded areas, where they remain during their first weeks of life. They retain their spots until about three months old.*

The fawn starts to eat solid foods at about two weeks of age and by four weeks, is strong enough to travel with its mother. At three months, it begins to lose its spots and takes on the coloration of adult deer. Fawns remain with their mothers through the first year and sometimes longer, forming a family group oriented around the doe.

## Age & Life Span

The average life span of a whitetail is between three and four years. However, they have been known to live up to 19 years.

The age of mature deer can be determined by a trained person examining the teeth in the lower jaw for replacement and

*Whitetails have a potential life span of up to 19 years, but most average three to four years. The forest has already reclaimed the remains of this buck.*

wear. The molars of whitetails wear down as they age. The teeth of deer may be completely worn out by seven years of age. A more accurate way of aging deer is to stain a thin section of tooth and then examine it under a microscope. Each year, a new ring appears between the layers of cementum in the root portion of the deer's tooth. The researcher simply counts these dark annual rings to determine the animal's age.

The age of deer 12 months and younger is easier to pin down. At six months, a deer's first molar is fully erupted and at nine months, its second molar has appeared. Among year-old deer, the third molar is usually partially erupted.

## Antlers

The antlers of bucks are of great interest to hunters, yet few know very much about them.

Antlers of the whitetail, as in other members of the deer family, are grown and shed each year. In many cases, large antlers enhance a buck's social rank among other males in the neighborhood, but a strong body is usually more important for establishing dominance. Fighting is most common between deer with similar-sized racks and is a means of these near-equals to establish dominance in the hierarchy.

*Antler growth, like so many things about the whitetail, is not perfectly under-stood. Biologists do know, however, that nutrition and genetics play important roles in the eventual size of a buck's antlers.*

Bucks shed their antlers after the breeding season. How long a buck keeps his antlers may depend on his nutritional condition. Generally, the better he eats, the longer he retains his antlers. New antlers may begin to grow right after the old ones are cast off; indeed, it is not uncommon to find that budding new antlers have pushed off the old pair.

The antlers stem from pedicles on the skull. They grow rapidly, reaching full size in 12 to 16 weeks. During the growing period, they are composed of a lattice-work of connective tissue covered by velvet, a skin-like covering that supplies blood to the antlers. Once fully formed, the tissue under the velvet solidifies into what we recognize as antlers and the velvet, no longer needed to supply nutrients to the growing tissue, is rubbed off. The buck rubs his antlers on bushes and small trees, gradually removing the velvet while polishing the tines.

The growth of antlers has fascinated and puzzled researchers for years. Why and how do they grow so fast? This has been of interest to people studying bone growth and particularly as it relates to the healing of fractures. What is the relationship between the fast-growing antler tissue and other fast-growing tissues, such as cancer cells? Why do some does develop antlers?

It is known that the size and shape of a buck's antlers, including the number of points, are determined by the quality and quantity of food, genetics, and hormonal regulation. There is some connection between a buck's age and the number of points

*Velvet supplies nutrients to the fast-growing antler tissue. Once the antlers reach full size, the blood vessels in the velvet begin to die. The velvet becomes dry, and starts to peel. The buck removes the dead skin by rubbing his antlers against trees and bushes.*

*Deformed antlers are often caused by injury to the animal during the antler-growing period.*

on his antlers, but it is not a reliable method for determining age. For example, in a healthy deer herd, 1½-year-old bucks may have antlers with as many as eight points. In a crowded condition, bucks from 1½ to 4½ years or older may have only small spikes. In an extremely crowded situation, bucks may not have any visible antlers.

Non-typical or abnormally-shaped antlers occur on some bucks. These distorted racks are attributed to several factors. Genetics is probably the most important; the genes which create unusual racks are passed along from one generation to the other. Castration or injury to the buck's reproductive system will also result in abnormal antler development. In addition, a deer injured on one side of its body may end up with a malformed antler on the opposite side.

## Home Range

The home range of whitetails has been and is the subject of considerable research. The latest findings indicate that deer in good habitat generally stay within a 300-acre range. But this changes throughout the year. Home ranges are generally smaller during the winter and largest in mid-summer. In autumn, a doe about to come into heat may pass through a buck's range and he will follow her until she is receptive. In addition, heavy hunting pressure or free-ranging dogs may push deer outside their normal home ranges.

## Habitat

Whitetails have very definite habitat requirements. They prefer wooded areas, especially hardwoods, with lots of borders or edges created by natural breaks between vegetative types or by fields or small clear-cuts. Referred to as the *edge effect* by biologists, this type of habitat provides a variety of foods and cover types. For example, in the more heavily-farmed sections of the country, deer feed on agricultural crops adjacent to woodlands. They use the woods primarily as resting and escape cover.

## Deer Beds

Knowing how to recognize and locate bedding areas is an important part of deer hunting. A bed is a pressed-down spot, about the size of a man, in leaves, grass, snow, or pine needles. Many stalk hunters touch the beds to see if they are still warm. If so, they know that deer are not far away.

The location of deer beds depends largely upon the season, weather, and hunting pressure. On warm days, deer that are not being hunted hard will bed on sunny slopes and near the edges of weedy fields. On cold, cloudy and windy days,they like to bed in dense evergreens or other cover that affords protection from the

*Whitetails usually bed in some type of cover where they can spot approaching danger quickly. Smart hunters locate bedding areas, then plan their hunting strategy accordingly.*

*Once alarmed, a fleeing whitetail wastes little time getting to cover. Sometimes they almost seem to disappear, as if swallowed up by the forest.*

elements. If hunting pressure is heavy, they often bed along the edge of a thicket where they can see what is approaching, but escape quickly into dense cover.

## Evasion Tactics

A spooked whitetail can run up to 40 miles per hour. If necessary, deer can run three miles or more at a speed of 20 miles per hour. And if that isn't enough, they can high jump an eight-foot fence and broad jump a 25-foot wide road.

But deer will also hold tight. It is difficult for hunters to imagine just how patient a whitetail buck can be when the hunting pressure is on. Once alerted, he can become a master of camouflage and concealment. Most hunters do not realize how often they walk by deer during the course of a season. Often within a few feet! The buck will exercise a tremendous amount of patience and remain hidden until the hunter walks past.

One hunter who can testify to the whitetail's stealth and trickery is Bob Good, nationally-known handgun hunter from Denver, Colorado. Bob and I were hunting in a swamp in the Deep South. While slipping along a logging road, Bob caught a glimpse of something shining beside a log some 150 yards away. Using his binoculars, he began studying the log carefully. What he discovered was a trophy-sized buck lying beside the log with his antlers laid back and his chin pressed to the ground. The enormous buck had spotted Bob and rather than running, had chosen to hide beside the log. He never got a shot at the magnificent animal, but just seeing the buck's evasion tactic was enjoyment enough.

In areas thickly populated with hunters, whitetails will often bed down in small thickets, allowing hunters to pass within a few feet. This behavior has been documented by researchers who have outfitted deer with radio collars, then used radio-telemetry equipment to track the animals. Once it gets dark, the deer move off to feed. But before the ensuing sunrise, they return to their hiding spots where they remain throughout the day. To overcome the whitetail's tendency to hang tight, the hunter would do well to use binoculars and spend more time looking and a lot less time walking.

Hunters should also remember that deer are excellent swimmers and that they do not hesitate to cross water. I have seen whitetails paddling between islands off the coast of Georgia. I have also watched deer swim a rather large river in Alabama on a regular basis. Many other biologists have seen deer feeding belly-deep on aquatic vegetation.

Deer will often swim beaver swamps and ponds, or wade creeks to escape hunters or dogs. Apparently they regard water as a sort of safety barrier. When scouting for deer, hunters should study streambanks for possible trails leading out of the water and up the bank. Many times deer will cross a river or creek, or come for water at the same place. Once you discover one of this spots, take a stand nearby.

The whitetail is one of the most fascinating creatures on earth. You can never learn too much about him. The more you learn, the better you will become at hunting this elusive animal. Take time to read everything you can. If you can spend some time with a wildlife biologist, pick his brain about the life cycle of deer and whitetail behavior. Get to know the whitetail like a good friend. With this kind of familiarity comes success.

# 2

# Whitetail Foods & Feeding

Hunters have many misconceptions about whitetail foods and feeding habits. Among the most prevalent are: deer feed only during early morning and late afternoon; they do not move to more abundant food within their territory; they eat only nuts; they are browsers, they never graze; they will come from miles around to lick a salt block; they can be easily shot at their watering holes; they require very little food for their size.

While some of these statements may hold a bit of truth under certain circumstances, they should not be considered as universal laws. Every hunter should learn the facts about deer foods and feeding patterns. Knowing this information can be extremely helpful in finding whitetails.

The foods and feeding habits of white-tailed deer vary from one area to another and from season to season. Whitetails are known to eat over 600 species of plants in North America. What they eat is based on what is available over their home range and is an instinctive search for the nutrients required for growth, lactation, reproduction, antler development, and to maintain body heat and strength.

To remain healthy, deer select a balanced diet from plants within their home range. They consume five to eight pounds of food per day for each 100 pounds of body weight.

*Author Fears (right), and noted archers Ben Rodgers Lee (left) and Fred Bear (center), examine several acorns, a primary deer food in many regions of the U.S. Both Ben Lee and Fred Bear have passed away since this photo was taken.*

In spring and summer, deer feed heavily on leaves, twigs, and low-growing plants such as grasses and forbs. In fall, many whitetails switch to fallen mast, primarily acorns. If the autumn mast crop is low, plants like honeysuckle and smilax (greenbrier) become more important.

Winter brings more complex changes to the world of the whitetail. On good range and under good conditions, the does and fawns continue to gain weight through December. The bucks are just trying to maintain their weight. January and February sees a reduction in the quantity and quality of food. But deer adapt to these environmental conditions by turning down their metabolism to conserve energy. Should winter come exceptionally early or last longer than normal in the spring, whitetails can be in serious trouble because their systems demand more nutrients than the habitat can supply.

Let's look at each food group and its importance to deer during the fall hunting season:

## Nuts & Fruits

Whitetails throughout the southern, eastern, and central regions of the United States feed heavily on white and red oak acorns during the fall. They also eat other types of mast including beechnuts, soft-shelled hickory nuts, and even pecans. Fruits, including wild persimmon, hawthorn, palmetto, and dogwood berries are also commonly eaten.

Acorns are low in protein, but high in carbohydrates, the best source of energy. When acorns are plentiful, deer are able to put on a few extra pounds, enhancing their ability to survive the rigors of winter and to produce additional fawns the following spring.

Oak trees reach 20 years of age before they begin producing acorns, and only a small percentage of the fruit ripens to maturity. The acorn drop usually occurs during October or November, though drought or strong winds may speed up the drop. Most acorns are eaten soon after they fall, but a few, especially those of red oaks may be available until spring. Weevil damage is often heavy, in some years up to 40 percent. Damaged acorns have less nutritional value, but are still consumed by deer.

*Leaves of red oak (left) are pointed with tiny bristles or spines; those of white oak (right) have rounded lobes.*

Whitetails seem to prefer the sweet-tasting acorns of white oak. I have watched deer walk through heavy drops of red oak acorns to feed on mast beneath a white oak. Because of the whitetail's fondness for white oak acorns, hunters should be able to distinguish between the two oak groups.

*White Oak.* This group includes bur oak, post oak, swamp oak, overcup oak, and white oak. The leaves have rounded, smooth lobes. The bark is gray to almost white, and scaly, often looking similar to hickory. The acorns mature in one growing season, are sweet to the taste, and the inner surface of the shell (not the cup) is smooth.

*Red Oak.* The group, also referred to as black oak, includes scarlet oak, pin oak, scrub oak, red oak, and other species. The leaves have pointed lobes tipped with bristles or thin spines. The bark is dark and furrowed. Acorns do not mature until the end of the second growing season, are bitter, and the inside of the shell is hairy.

### Herbaceous Plants

Non-woody, or herbaceous plants, are extremely important to deer in the fall. Deer graze on a variety of broadleaved species

*Whitetails graze on a wide variety of low-growing herbaceous plants including grasses, sedges, and legumes. During winter, they spend more time browsing on woody plants.*

including grasses, sedges, and various kinds of legumes, asters, and ferns. Herbaceous plants often emerge in profusion following a forest or range fire. These areas become lush cafeterias that attract large concentrations of deer. Some of the best hunting I've found has been on one-year-old burns, where herbaceous plants were abundant. The plants also thrive along roads, forest openings, powerline corridors, and field edges.

## Woody Plants

Deer eat the leaves and flowering portions of woody plants throughout the growing season. After the leaf fall, the dormant plants offer little nutrition for deer. Whitetails turn to woody stems and twigs, called *browse*, only when other sources of food are unavailable or when other foods are of poorer quality.

The list of woody plants eaten by whitetails nationwide would be several pages long; here is a sampling of foods from different regions:

Northern states and southern Canada—maples, dogwood, aspen, blueberries, honeysuckle, yew, and ground hemlock.

Southern states—greenbrier, poison ivy, blackgum, honeysuckle, and dogwood.

Western states—sumac, wild plum, bearberry, buckbush, poplar, and chokecherry.

## Mushrooms

A number of mushrooms and other types of fungi are relished by deer. The highly-nutritious fungi may help to compensate for nutrient deficiencies in other foods. Many species of mushrooms that are deadly to man are apparently harmless to wildlife, including deer. In the Deep South, mushrooms become particularly important to whitetails during winter, when their food needs are critical.

## Agricultural Crops

Clover, alfalfa, corn, winter wheat, oats, soybeans, peas, sweet potatoes, and apples are only a few of many agricultural crops that attract deer. Farm crops are especially important after acorns are consumed and may be the only winter foods available to whitetails in some areas. In the Cornbelt states, entire herds of deer move into fields of standing corn. The tall stalks provide excellent cover and the rows are easy avenues for finding food and escaping danger.

*Hayfields with alfalfa and clover attract large concentrations of deer. Wildlife managers may have to control specific animals when they become a nuisance.*

Crops that remain green through winter, such as oats, rye, winter wheat, alfalfa, and clover often draw large numbers of deer. Whitetails are also attracted to farm crops that have just been fertilized. In some regions, deer cause so much damage that farmers can no longer afford to plant certain types of crops.

### Water

The water requirements of deer depend on the season of the year. In winter, whitetails usually require about 1½ quarts for every 100 pounds of body weight on a daily basis. In summer, when temperatures are warmer and whitetails more active, they need two to three quarts per 100 pounds.

Whitetails will seek out and drink water, but can usually obtain enough from their food, most of which is 50 to 90 percent water. In winter, deer can meet their water requirements by eating snow or licking ice if they cannot find open water.

### Salt

Deer, like all living things, require certain minerals to remain healthy. Salt, however, may not be one of them. Still, there is no doubt that whitetails relish the taste of salt, particularly in early summer. Deer visit natural salt licks, salt blocks in pastures, and roads that have been salted to melt ice. They will even frequent sites where smokehouses and outhouses once stood, licking or eating the salty soil.

## Feeding Habits

Deer feed the heaviest in early morning or just before dark, and if left relatively undisturbed, they will also feed lightly during midday. However, there are many exceptions to this general feeding pattern. For example, when hunting pressure is heavy, they will stay hidden during the day and feed at night. On bright, moonlit nights, deer may feed all night and move very little during the day. They also begin feeding later in the day on moonlit evenings.

Whitetails have a way of knowing when bad weather or a cold front is on the way. They will feed heavily, often throughout the day, some 12 to 24 hours before the system reaches them. When the storm hits, they bed down and wait it out, often not feeding for several days. Once the weather breaks, they quickly catch up on their eating. Deer in a light rain with little wind usually follow normal feeding patterns.

*At this natural salt lick, whitetails paw up and then eat the salty soil.*

*Whitetails frequent edges where they can find an abundance of food.*

Bucks in the rut eat very little. If you are hunting during the peak of the rut, forget about trying to ambush a feeding buck. He has only sex on his mind; eating is low on his list of priorities.

By now, you can see that the study of deer foods and feeding habits is somewhat complicated, but nonetheless an essential part of the serious hunter's education. Deer foods vary tremendously as do their feeding habits, but if you can put it all together, you'll be rewarded with your own tasty food for the table.

# 3

# How to Use a
# Topographic Map

You were lucky to have your name drawn for a special two-
day deer hunt on military land in a neighboring state. Since
this hunt will be on land that is otherwise closed, you have been
unable to scout the terrain.

The first morning of the hunt finds you in line, long before
daylight, with all the other chosen hunters. As you wait for the
checking station to open, you wonder where and how you will
hunt this strange land. The map provided by the military shows
only the various roads criss-crossing the area—little else is
shown. You even have some thoughts about the possibility of
getting lost, but you know that won't happen if you hunt close to
a road.

Growing restless, you walk up to the car ahead to see if other
hunters know any more than you do. As you draw near, you can
see the occupants, with the dome light on, looking at a large,
green-colored map. You hear one of the hunters comment on the
probability of deer trails on the sloping north side of Settlers'
Ridge. Then, one of the hunters explains how he plans to walk
along an abandoned tank road, where he is sure to find scrapes.

You stop and wonder. No one was allowed to scout this
area, so how do they know so much about it? Do they know a
general or have political pull? These guys know exactly where
they are going.

The other hunters were not given special treatment, but they do have one big advantage over you—a topographic map and the knowledge of how to use it. Before the hunt, the group spent several nights studying the map, then applied what each hunter knew about deer habits. By doing this, they were able to plan their hunt, even though none of the hunters had ever set foot on the land.

Today, almost all areas of the U.S. have been topographically mapped by the U.S. Geological Survey (U.S.G.S.), a division of the Department of the Interior. These topographic maps are a graphic representation of natural and man-made features on the earth's surface, plotted to a definite scale. The most distinguishing characteristic of the maps is that they show the shape and elevation of the terrain. They reveal the location and shape of mountains, valleys, plains, streams, lakes, ravines, and the works of man including roads, buildings, powerline corridors, etc.

Topographic maps, or *topo maps* as they are frequently called, are made from a quadrangle unit of survey which is bound in parallels of latitude and meridians of longitude. The topos of most help to sportsmen are quadrangles covering 7½ minutes of latitude and longitude, and published at a scale of 1:24,000, or one inch equals 2,000 feet.

Each map is designated by the name of a city, town, community, or prominent natural feature within its borders. The name is in bold letters in the lower right corner. If the area you are interested in covers more than one map, look for the names of adjoining topos on the margin of your map. The 7½-minute series map only covers from 49 to 70 square miles, so it is often necessary to obtain several other maps.

Topo maps are usually printed in four colors—black for man-made features, blue for water areas, green for woodlands, and brown contour lines that depict relief features such as mountains and valleys. Be sure to request a *woodland overprint* on your topo map.

The process of ordering topo maps is relatively simple. First, write the U.S. Geological Survey (Federal Center, Box 25286, Denver, CO 80225 or call 800-USA-MAPS) for an index of maps for your state. Once you receive the index, find the area, stream, etc., in which you are interested. It will have one or more black squares over it with names printed in the square. The name in each square is the name of a map. Write the appropriate U.S. Geological Survey office and request the maps by name, series

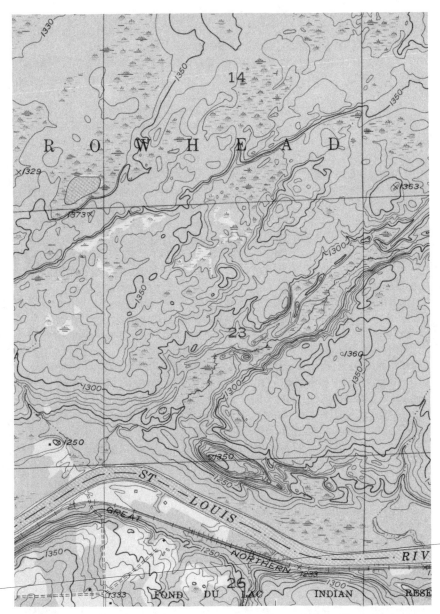

*Detail from a topographic map (actual size) shows a variety of natural features including a small lake, river and stream, marshland, and steep ridges. Man-made features include houses, roads, trails, and railroad grade. The map's green woodland overprint shows up as gray in this reproduction. White areas depict fields and clearings in the woods.*

and state. For instance, a map order might be: "One copy of Mays Lick, 7½-minute series, Kentucky, with woodland overprint."

Because topo maps are updated only every few years, you may have to add a few recent man-made features such as roads or reservoirs. Look for the survey date under the map name in the lower right corner.

A map, like a compass, is no better or worse than the person using it. It behooves you to learn how to read a topo map. This can be easily done by purchasing a map of a familiar area near your home. Take the map and drive the roads. Relate the map symbols to on-the-ground features, both man-made and natural. Next, walk a distance cross-country, up a hill, or down into a valley or creek bottom. Study the map's contour lines and relate them to the rise and fall of the land. Think of the contour line as an imaginary line on the ground, which takes any shape necessary to maintain a constant elevation.

If you look closely at the contour lines, you will see that every fourth or fifth contour, depending on the contour interval, will be printed in a heavier line. This line is known as the *index contour*. Along this contour you will find the elevation printed at given intervals. The elevation at any point can be determined by finding an index contour line and counting each contour line to your desired point. The contour interval at the bottom center of the map, under the scale, tells you the elevation change between these contour lines. The closer the lines, the steeper the terrain; the farther apart, the flatter the landscape.

Learn to use your map's scale so you can estimate distances and walking time to hunting or camping areas. On the 7½-minute series topo, each 2⅝ inches equals one mile.

In short, the U.S.G.S. topo map enables you to sit at the kitchen table and look down on your planned hunting area. Once you have learned to read the map, put knowledge of deer behavior and habitat to work and plan your outing on the map. This procedure will save time and improve your odds for success. Now let's see how the topo map can make you a more successful hunter.

## Case 1

*Situation:* You arrive at a deer hunting camp the night before opening day. You are a guest of the eight hunters who use this camp and you have never been here before. The camphouse is at the flowing well marked on your topo map. You talk to the hunters during supper and find out several things:

***Hunter records the location of a fresh scrape on his topo map.***

1.   They plan to hunt the swamp along the river due south of camp. Most will be stalk hunting.

2.   They rarely hunt north of the camp anymore, because of the large clear-cut area three-fourths of a mile due north, along a small unnamed creek. They claim that the logging operation two years ago scared away all the deer and there are no more mast trees left to provide food for deer.

3.   There is a raised railroad bed running southwest from the camp. It was used back in the 1920s to haul logs out of the swamp.

4.   The bucks are in the peak of their rut.

*Solution No. 1:* After supper, you have a few minutes alone to plan your hunt, so you get out your topo map and locate the camp. Next, you call one of the guys over to help you draw in the clear-cut area. Since the bucks are in full rut, you know that if you look in the right places you will eventually find some fresh scrapes. Since everyone else is going into the swamp, you will avoid that area. You remember that bucks like to make their scrapes along old field edges, thinly-forested ridgetops, and old roads. You decide to leave camp the next morning on a route that will take you along one edge of the clear-cut, across the ridgetop to the west of camp, and down the old railroad bed. You mark your map accordingly, and turn in.

**Topographic maps can be invaluable aids for all types of hunting, whether you use a muzzleloader, rifle, or bow and arrow.**

The next morning you arrive at the clear-cut at daybreak and find plenty of deer sign, but no scrapes. You move south across the ridges, but they are thickly forested and void of scrapes. Next, you walk down off the ridge and hit the railroad bed. Bingo! It's mid-morning and you have found four well-worked scrapes. You pick a stand where you can see two of the scrapes, sprinkle a few drops of deer scent on each scrape, and get comfortable. By 3 p.m. you are heading back to camp along the railroad grade to get someone to help you haul your six-pointer back to camp.

*Solution No. 2:* But suppose the rut hasn't started? You know that your host hunters were wrong about no deer being in the clear-cut. In fact, there is usually much more browse in a two-year-old clear-cut than in the woods. You leave camp and arrive at the cutover area before sunrise. The night before, you picked out a hilltop on your map which should provide a good view of the entire area. You find the hill and take a stand. That morning, several deer come and go off to your right, but nothing close. During the middle of the day, you ease around to where you saw the deer. Sure enough, there is a well-worn trail entering the clear-cut from a brushy area between two small creeks. You take a stand on a downed treetop that affords a view of the area. At dusk, three does ease into the clear-cut and seconds later, a huge 10-pointer emerges from cover to begin feeding with the does.

## Case 2

*Situation:* You are scouting a few days before deer season opens and marking your findings on a topo map.

*Solution:* As you scout out your hunting territory, keep a record of all fresh sign on your map. If you find beds, mark the general area, because deer seldom bed in the same spot each day. Next, mark choice feeding areas. You may have to study the feeding habits of deer to do this. Find deer trails that connect these areas. Watch for fresh droppings and tracks. Try to pick stands where fresh, well-used trails come together. As you record the information on your map, likely stand-hunting sites will become apparent. Mark your stands on the map, then use a compass to find them on opening day.

On your topo map, you should have marked some bedding areas. Trails from these spots remain separate until they cross a creek, where they come together—a good stand site. Then they branch out, merging again at the edge of a grove of white oaks, a choice feeding area. Here is a second good stand. A third site would be just inside the oak grove. Now you have an excellent plan for yourself and two buddies to follow on opening day.

Almost any species of game can be hunted more successfully if you follow a marked topo map. It puts you into the best habitat and keeps you from wasting time wandering around in poor areas. By using a compass with your map, you can go right to the best habitat in short order.

These are but a few of the many ways a topo map can help the sportsman. The more you use them, the more you will depend on them for enjoyable hunting, fishing, and camping trips.

# 4

# Scouting for Whitetails

If there is one thing that can change whitetail hunting from pure luck to calculated success, it's scouting. Game officials who manage hunting areas say that as many as 75 percent of the hunters park their cars, walk a few yards into the woods, then sit down and wait for a big buck to come by. That's luck. The other 25 percent spend some time before the season finding a specific spot to hunt. They reduce the odds by discovering the location of deer and choosing the best way to hunt them. When these hunters get a deer, it's calculated success—the result of thorough scouting.

Basically, pre-season scouting answers one big question: "Do I know for sure there are deer in the area I plan to hunt?"

If you hunt on public land, it is wise to start scouting in early fall. Once you have decided on a specific tract of land, your first step is to order your index of topographic maps and from that, a topo of the area. When the map arrives, study it carefully until you have a good picture of the terrain. Be sure to take your map along on scouting trips and mark the spots where you find deer sign. The map will also prove invaluable for finding your stand or stalk hunting area on opening morning.

Your next step should be to visit someone familiar with the deer habitat in your hunting area. If your spot is in a national forest, visit the district ranger; if it's a public hunting area, see the area wildlife manager or biologist; if you're on pulp or paper company land, check with the woodlands management office; or if it's privately owned, visit the state game biologist for that section or the Soil Conservation Service officer assigned to that county. These officials are aware of habitat conditions and can provide a wealth of information to help you be successful.

During your visit, ask the official about the quality of the habitat. What are deer feeding on most heavily during hunting season? Has it been a good year for mast production? If so, get him to explain which trees produce the best deer food and where they are located. If it happens to be a poor year for mast, what are deer eating instead? Where is that food in your hunting area? Get a clear understanding of what deer are eating and be sure you know how to identify the food plants. Don't be afraid to admit that you cannot recognize smilax or some other plant. Ask to see samples or pictures of plants that are unfamiliar to you.

Encourage the official to share any other information regarding deer and deer movement in your hunting area. Many times these authorities can give you tips on trail locations, bedding areas, and feeding periods.

Once you have gathered all this data, you may want to scout your hunting area a month or more before the deer season. On this scouting trip, concentrate primarily on learning the terrain, identifying food plants, and locating possible bedding and feeding areas.

Your more serious scouting should be as close to opening day as possible. Deer have a way of changing habits just before the hunting season opens. They begin switching from late summer to fall foods. Colder days mean that bedding areas will change. The rut is coming on and the bucks are becoming restless and covering more ground. The later you scout, the more accurate and up-to-date your findings will be, increasing your chances of being in the right place at the right time on opening morning.

Take your scouting trips seriously. Go into your woods before daylight and observe deer movement. Stay late and watch for movement again that afternoon. Of course, the best sign you can find is actually seeing the animals. If you spot deer, determine what they were eating and the direction they were moving. Mark these findings on your map. If the deer were using a trail, follow it, and draw it on your map. Make drawings of all other trails you find.

## Deer Foods

Observe the deer's food supply as you walk. An area of planted pine with little or no underbrush will probably not have enough food to keep deer in the area. Learn what deer are eating and make sure the land has an ample food supply. If you find a particularly good source of food, such as a grove of white oaks loaded with acorns, mark it on your map. Do any of the deer trails lead into the grove? If so, you have discovered a system that spells success.

## Tracks

Watch for tracks. You can tell fresh tracks in damp ground because the side of the tracks will be moist. Old tracks will be dry on the inside. Fresh tracks in dry ground will have sharp edges and will not be filled in by leaves or dirt.

*On damp ground, the edges of fresh tracks are moist.*

Don't waste your time trying to distinguish the deer's sex by its tracks. Contrary to popular belief, you can't tell the difference. Large tracks, or those which show the dew claws, may be made by any running or heavy whitetails. And don't be misled by the number of tracks. Deer usually take short steps, so one whitetail can leave a lot of tracks. On the other hand, if you don't find any tracks, especially along abandoned logging roads, in the soft dirt between rows of corn, or other places where tracks show up readily, beware. If deer are in the area and the ground is reasonably soft, you should find tracks.

**Droppings**

Droppings are another certain sign of deer. The droppings of whitetails come in two basic shapes, round and oblong. Rabbit and porcupine droppings are similar, but usually smaller and more fibrous. Fresh deer droppings are glistening black and moist for the first few hours. Older droppings are dull and dry

*Fresh droppings appear shiny black and moist.*

*Whitetail bucks rub small trees to remove velvet from their antlers. Bucks also rub a gland just above their eye, leaving scent to mark their territories.*

looking. Finding several piles of droppings is a good sign, but don't get overly excited and start thinking the place is loaded with deer. Biologists say that each whitetail deposits up to a dozen piles of droppings a day.

## Scrapes and Rubs

If you are scouting during the rut, fresh rubs and scrapes are proof positive that you are in a buck's territory. At the beginning of the rut, a buck will move around his territory and begin to rub his antlers on small saplings. These scarred trees are called *rubs*. At the same time, he will start leaving his calling card in the form of a pawed-out spot on the ground. He makes these *scrapes* by using his front foot to dig out leaves, grass, and twigs. Then he uses his foot and sometimes his antlers to stir up the soil. Next, he will urinate in the fresh dirt to leave his scent.

Almost all scrapes have overhanging branches some three to four feet off the ground. After urinating in the pawed dirt, the buck will reach up and chew on the branches to leave even more scent. Every few hours he will check all his scrapes and re-freshen them.

Does in heat look for scrapes. If they find one, they urinate on the spot and then wait in the area for the buck to show up. Also, rival bucks will urinate in the scrapes, either as a warning or perhaps a challenge.

Bucks like to make their scrapes on the fringes of their terri-tories. The rutting buck usually picks an open area such as the border of an abandoned field, the edge of a feeding site, along an old logging road or a sparsely-wooded ridgetop. The buck will work the scrape from a minimum of once every three days to a maximum of several times a day.

When you find scrapes, make sure they are active. Look for freshly-turned dirt. The soil will have a strong urine odor and the overhanging branches will be chewed. If you find these clues, you are onto an old buck. Mark the scrapes on your map, because they will make excellent spots to stand hunt.

## Beds

As you scout the area, be alert for bedding areas. Often, trails leading into feeding sites come from bedding areas. Remember, during fall and winter, deer will bed regularly in the same general area, unless constantly disturbed by hunters.

If you have done a thorough job of scouting, deciding where and how to hunt will be easy. In fact, you have already marked several good stands or stalk hunting areas, which answers the *where*. *How* to hunt is up to you. Using the information you found while scouting, select the method which you think will work best or the technique you enjoy the most. Then, leave the road-sitters behind and get yourself a buck.

# 5

# The Art of Stalk Hunting

One of the most effective methods of hunting white-tailed deer is also one of the most misunderstood. This technique is commonly called *stalk hunting*, though in some regions it is also referred to as still hunting.

Thousands of sportsmen call themselves stalk hunters, but only a small fraction really understands and practices the true art of stalk hunting. While it's not a complicated skill to learn, it requires a tremendous amount of patience and a keen awareness of yourself and your surroundings. Because many hunters lack these traits and don't have the self-discipline to learn them, their stalk hunting is nothing more than a hurried stroll through the woods.

To learn the art of stalk hunting, one must first understand the simple theory behind the method. It involves torturously slow movement through good deer habitat, taking only a few well-placed steps at a time, then stopping for five minutes or more. You spend more time looking, listening, and blending in with the surroundings than you do moving. Sounds easy, doesn't it? It is, *if* you follow a few basics.

## Pre-Season Scouting

Pre-season scouting is a must, just as it is for any other type of deer hunting. Try to scout the area just before your hunt and bring along a topo map, so you can record signs like rubs, scrapes, trails and crossings, feeding and bedding areas. Also, mark dry creek beds, logging roads, fire breaks, old fields, and other features that might prove helpful. Get to know the land you plan to hunt. Your map should also have alternate routes for different conditions, such as wind direction, the dryness of the woods, etc. Stalk hunting, like any other type of hunt, should be well-planned before you leave home.

Wear a blaze orange vest and hat when stalk hunting, since you are covering a fair amount of ground. Nearly all states and provinces require some orange or red clothing. I feel much safer wearing blaze orange and I don't think it has cut down on my effectiveness.

I wear an old pair of hunting boots with soles that are worn thin. The thin bottoms allow me to feel the ground much better than soles that are thick or cleated. However, some hunters prefer thin, gummy-type soles for quiet walking.

Be sure to get into the woods well before daylight. This gives you time to determine the direction of your stalk. If possible, walk with the sun at your back and the wind in your face. The advantages are obvious: whitetails will not be able to pick up your scent and the sun will illuminate any movement or white patch of hair. Deer are much easier to see if the sun is shining on any of

*Well-worn boots enable hunters to "feel" the ground and to move stealthily.*

their white parts. But if you have to make a choice, wind direction should be your most important consideration.

If all goes well, you should be able to walk with the wind blowing in your face. Still, it is advisable to sprinkle some type of masking scent on your hunting coat, trouser legs, and boots. The best place to douse it on your boots is along the seam between the sole and the upper part of the boot.

When the woods are wet from rain, moving quietly may not be a problem. But in a dry woods, it is almost impossible to walk quietly over the leaves. If this is the case, use old logging roads, dry creek beds, fire breaks, or utility rights-of-way as trails. These areas usually have fewer leaves and twigs, enabling you to walk more quietly.

If you are stalk hunting in snow, try to avoid crusty spots. A fresh snow is best. You can move quietly and visibility is often excellent. When stalking in snow, try to move from tree to tree and stop in shadows. If you come upon fresh tracks going in your direction, follow them. You may catch up to a trophy.

**The Stalk Hunting Technique**

Perhaps the most important rule in stalk hunting is to keep your movement to a minimum. If you take more than five or six steps at a time, you are moving too fast. If you are seeing only the flags of whitetails, you are definitely moving too fast and spooking the animals into flight. And, you are not watching carefully enough.

Many beginning hunters want to know how much ground they should cover in an hour of stalk hunting. A good rule of thumb is to walk no more than one-quarter of a mile in an hour. But many veteran hunters would consider this running. These old pros move so slowly that they seldom cover more than two miles per day.

As you walk, slowly transfer your weight from one foot to the other, so you're never off-balance. This allows you to freeze instantly. Plan each step. When choosing where you will place your next step, take advantage of moss-covered areas, rock outcrops, packed dry mud, sand, or anything that you can safely walk on, yet will be quiet underfoot. If possible, avoid loose gravel, sticks, dry leaves, etc., or you will alert every animal in the woods.

If you must cross a patch of dry leaves, do so in three or four quick steps. This sounds much like the quick hops of a squirrel feeding along the ground. Study the sounds a squirrel makes in

*Take advantage of large trees to break up your outline.*

dry leaves and learn to imitate them. If the wind is gusting, move only when the wind blows. This will help cover your noise as well as movement.

As you move, try to end each series of steps so you are standing next to a tree or bush. These natural features will break up your outline. Always hold your rifle in a vertical position, as vertical lines are more natural to deer. Also, avoid stalk hunting on ridgetops. Deer looking up at a hunter moving along the skyline will spook easily. Instead, walk several feet below the crest of the ridge. Rather than walking through a sparse woods, skirt the edge. Always keep your background in mind and don't stand out.

Perhaps the most trying part of stalk hunting is the long period of looking and listening at each stop. Be patient. Stay put for at least five minutes. Slowly study everything to the front and sides. Occasionally look behind you, but remember to turn your head ever-so-slowly. You can never tell if a deer may be watching you.

One of the hardest skills to teach beginning stalk hunters is "what to look for." Learn to look for parts of deer, because you will rarely spot the whole animal. Watch for the tip of an ear, the shine off an eye, or the flick of a tail. Many times, especially during the rut, sunlight shining on polished antlers will give away the hiding spot of a buck. Carefully study everything in sight. What looks like a large, gray rock may, in fact, be a hiding whitetail with its head pressed to the ground. If you are stalking through dense woods, occasionally stoop down and look below the brush line. You'll be surprised by how far you can see. You may suddenly notice four legs that don't belong there.

Keep your ears tuned to all noises. If you hear something you can't readily identify, stop and study the situation. Deer make many sounds. A cracking noise may be a buck feeding on acorns; a grunting sound might be a rutting buck; something walking over dry leaves might be one or more deer moving your way. To the experienced hunter, each noise is a puzzle to be solved.

If the wind is right and you are moving slowly enough, deer won't know you are nearby. They will be calmly going about their business. By keeping a sharp eye for any movement, regardless of how slight, you can often spot deer before they spot you.

When you see deer, freeze. Observe their direction of movement. If the deer is in range, slowly get into shooting position when he is not looking in your direction. If he is out of range for

*Squat down occasionally to peer below the brush line. If you see a deer, freeze. Determine the direction it is moving before you edge into shooting position.*

your bow or gun, but moving toward you, remain perfectly still until he moves close enough. Many stalk hunters have bucks walk to within a few feet of them.

If a deer is moving away from you, stalk toward the animal at the same slow pace. Don't get too anxious and begin walking faster. If he hasn't seen you, chances are he will move slowly and stop to feed occasionally, allowing you to gain ground. He may even bed down nearby. Needless to say, this can be a nerve-racking experience, but the thrill of a lifetime.

Walking near or through an old weedy field may allow you to catch a whitetail in its bed. Stop at the edge of the field and study every foot of it carefully. Again, look for parts of an animal—an eye, antlers, etc. If you must cross the field, move slowly and be alert. Often deer will lie low in their bed and hope you pass by without seeing them. They will do the same thing when bedded in wooded areas.

If you jump a deer, stop and remain motionless for several minutes. Many times, if a young deer is not frightened too badly, it will return to see what scared it. Twice I have had good bucks return to investigate what startled them. They made a wide circle and came back to where I was stooped down. Curiosity got the best of them.

Other things to consider when stalk hunting include:

• Don't grab or lean against saplings. Small trees, when moved a little at shoulder height, move a lot above your head. On a still day, it's like waving a flag to point out your position.

• When crossing a creek, wade quietly. Don't splash across. This is a frightening sound in a quiet woods.

• Wear clothing made from quiet, soft material like cotton, wool, or polyester blends. A nylon jacket can be noisy when slipping through thick underbrush and briars.

• It is possible to stalk close enough for a shot if you pick your time to move. Edge forward when the animal is feeding with its head down, when its head is behind a tree or bush, or when it is turned away from you. Take advantage of any cover between you and the animal, and when you get a chance, move from cover to cover. When the deer looks your way, freeze.

Stalk hunting, like any other method of hunting whitetails, requires some effort and a lot of experience. However, once mastered, it can be one of the most thrilling and successful techniques of all.

# 6

# Stand Hunting

Hunters have long debated the attributes of hunting from a stand as opposed to stalk hunting. However, a situation that occurred while I was preparing this chapter reminded me of just how valuable stand hunting can be to the hunter.

I was guiding a group of hunters out of my Stagshead Lodge in west-central Alabama. One morning, a hunter asked if he could stalk hunt a long creek bottom that has typically been home for several bucks. I agreed with him that a slow stalk hunt could be very productive. The next morning, he was in the creek bottom long before daylight. He hunted the entire area until about noon without seeing a deer. But he did find a great deal of sign.

Three mornings later, a new hunter asked to work the same area. He was an experienced hunter, so I felt his odds were good for producing a fine buck. At noon, when I drove my four-wheel-drive to the bridge to pick him up, he was wearing a wide grin on his face. At his feet was a handsome four-point buck of generous proportions. The hunter enthusiastically related his success story.

Shortly after daylight, he had spotted an old permanent stand in a birch tree. Recognizing that the vegetation was thick along the creek, he decided to spend the morning in the tree stand. He had been there for less than an hour when the heavy forkhorn came through the thicket. The rest of the story was lying at his feet.

A few mornings later, a third hunter requested to stalk hunt the same area. When I picked him up, he was empty-handed. He had jumped several bucks, but the creek bottom was so thick that all he could see were the flags of escaping deer.

Two days passed and no one hunted the area. Finally, a fourth hunter approached me. Again, this was an experienced hunter who I felt could put down a nice buck. When I picked him up at the bridge, his story was the same as the second hunter. He hollered very excitedly, "Fears, I'd sure appreciate it if you'd go back up there to an old tree stand I found and help me drag out a five-pointer." This hunter had spotted the same tree stand early in the morning and from it, had shot the animal.

The lesson we can learn from these experiences is that stand hunting has a definite place in deer hunting. And, in certain situations, it can be even more effective than stalk hunting.

### Pre-season Scouting

The first step in learning how to stand hunt is knowing how to pick a location. Far too many hunters walk a short distance into the woods, pick the first tree that looks any good, and set up their stand. By noon, they're wondering why they haven't seen a deer. Stand hunting is simple, but not that simple. To see deer, you must get to an area that has whitetails and where the odds are in your favor.

If possible, spend as much time as you can scouting before the season opens. Get to know the terrain as well as you know your back yard. Once you get a feel for the lay of the land, start to collect all the information you can about deer habitat. Spend some time talking with a biologist or other conservation official that knows the area. Ask him the questions outlined in the scouting chapter (page 33).

Once you've collected your information, return to the hunting spot a week before the season. Deer movements and feeding habits change with the season and the food supply, so it would be unwise to look for stand sites too early. An example is a situation where a hunter scouted an area in August. The deer were moving into the creek bottoms to feed on honeysuckle. He selected a stand accordingly. When he returned in November, he didn't see a deer because they were feeding on white oak acorns along the ridges.

On this final scouting trip, be systematic in locating your stands. Don't make the mistake many stand hunters make—selecting the first stand they find that enables them to look out over a large amount of territory.

Begin your scouting by locating food plants. Keep a record on your topo map. Once you find an ample supply of food, look for tracks and fresh droppings. If there is a lot of sign and the food supply is abundant, you may want to consider a stand in or near the feeding site. Many successful stand hunters set up only in areas with choice deer food like groves of white oak that have dropped a large supply of acorns.

Next, look for trails leading to these feeding areas. These well-worn trails often connect one food supply with another, but more often they lead from feeding areas to bedding sites. In hilly country, bucks like to bed down on brushy slopes, usually near the heads of creeks or ravines. In flat country, they prefer thick creek bottoms. From these secluded areas, they move each day and/or night to the food source. Record the trails on your map.

*This stand hunter is smelling for urine in the soil of a scrape.*

If you find a heavily-used trail, you may want to consider a stand along the route.

You may find a spot where several trails come together. It may be at a choice feeding area, a low saddle between two steep ridges, or at a stream crossing. If you find such an intersection and there is ample sign like fresh droppings, tracks, or slides (where deer have slid down a stream bank), you have found an excellent location for a stand. Deer movement is often concentrated at an intersection, so you have a good chance of seeing more than one animal.

Your basic scouting is complete once you have selected one or more stand sites. But before you return home, re-visit the site you plan to use on opening morning. Select several exact spots, or if you use a portable tree stand, several trees. Remember, you will be returning in the dark, yet you must be able to find each site quickly and with as little effort as possible. The wind may be blowing from almost any direction on opening morning, forcing you to switch to another stand. Nothing is more frustrating than to be on stand at daylight and find that the wind is carrying your scent toward the deer trail. It can be equally frustrating to have the rising sun in your face, making it difficult to see.

As you select your alternate sites, think of the various ways the wind might blow, the direction of the sun at sunrise, and your field of view. It is better to break sticks out of your stand on a scouting trip than on opening morning.

Another point to remember is to avoid stands on ridgetops. There, you would be silhouetted against the sky and your every movement would be easily seen by deer. Put yourself in the place of a deer and evaluate your stands. This will help you locate spots where you will become a part of the woods and not a strange object to be avoided. Make use of fallen trees and thickets. It is always good to have a tree to your back, both for comfort and to break up your outline.

### Portable Tree Stands

Often in my deer-hunting seminars, novice hunters ask why it is advantageous to hunt from a tree stand. My answer usually turns into a two or three-hour lecture. Tree stands offer a number of definite advantages over ground blinds. First, the hunter's scent remains above the animal or in a small area surrounding his stand. Being cautious of the wind direction and wearing a cover scent assures you of seeing more game.

*Whitetails will sometimes walk directly beneath a hunter in a tree stand.*

Another benefit is concealment. Many deer will pass near the tree stand and never look at the human mass perched above their eye level. Occasionally a deer might look up and spot the hunter, especially if he does not remain still. However, the conscientious hunter who places his tree stand some 12 to 20 feet above the ground has a decided advantage over any deer that walk by. (Some states have height limits for placing man-made tree stands. Also, tree stands may not be allowed on some lands owned by timber companies.)

*Many hunters prefer permanent tree stands (left) that are large enough so they can be more comfortable throughout the day. Portable tree stands (right) offer the hunter mobility.*

If legal, situating your tree stand high above ground affords a good view of the surrounding area. Where the cover is extremely thick, such as creeks with cane bottoms, swamps with lots of alder and willow, dense palmetto, groups of conifers, and other areas that would be almost impossible to hunt from the ground, the hunter in a portable tree stand can select a well-positioned tree, then look down into the cover.

The elevated stand also gives the hunter an opportunity to observe deer unspooked, enabling him to make a clean kill. This is important to those who enjoy tasty venison. The majority of animals taken from a tree stand do not see the hunter and are unalarmed. This assures the hunter of getting a good shot at an animal that is moving slowly.

Being perched on a tree stand does restrict your movement, which can be to your advantage. The hunter who has little room in which to twitch and move has less chance of being noticed by deer. The ground hunter who is stretching, sitting down, standing up, and walking around often reveals his location long before he ever sees the animals.

The tree stand instills patience in many hunters who normally lack it, and that may be one of the most important keys to killing big bucks. Once you have gone to the trouble of erecting your stand, climbing up the tree and getting situated, you are more likely to stay put for long periods than someone who is free to move about on the ground. This alone has forced many hunters to exercise patience, resulting in more success.

Some of the disadvantages of tree stand hunting are quite obvious. Putting up a portable tree stand can make a lot of noise. You may, in fact, startle deer in the immediate area for a short time. However, it has been my experience that whitetails do not stay frightened for long, nor do they move very far away. Several times I have barely climbed into my tree stand, attached my safety belt and sat down, when a deer suddenly appeared within bow range. This has led me to believe that the animal was nearby and my sounds did not bother him at all. In fact, it may have been attracted by the noise—remember, deer are curious.

Another disadvantage of tree stands is that they can be extremely cold places to hunt on frigid days. However, you can overcome the cold by wearing clothing that is designed for hunting in winter. Dress to be warm. If you are unbearably cold, you will find it impossible to remain still for any length of time.

Many hunters complain about toting a heavy tree stand into the woods. Granted, a 20- to 30-pound portable stand can be a chore to carry. To overcome the problem, I try to be very thorough while scouting, pinpointing the spot where I want my stand, then selecting the most direct route to the area. I often hunt on private land where I know that few, if any, other hunters will be around. In this instance, I leave my stand on the tree for the duration of the hunt. I tried this on public hunting areas, but once had a tree stand stolen, even though I locked it to the tree. Be sure to check on the legality of leaving your stand in the woods.

## Choosing a Site

Selecting a good tree for stand hunting is not always easy. First, do not use one that is leaning, crooked, dead, or one that has low limbs or a large base, such as a cypress. Choosing the

*Toting a tree stand can be a chore, but shoulder straps make it easier. Choose the most direct route from your vehicle to the stand site.*

wrong tree can cause problems. Years ago, I was guiding a hunter who had just purchased a new tree stand. I showed him an area with several bucks and turned him loose. Late that afternoon I saw him waving from a road in the area. When I got to the hunter, he looked like he'd been in a fight with a bear. He had selected a cypress tree for his tree stand, not noticing that the higher he climbed, the smaller the trunk became. He got up to 30 feet where the tree was too small for the adjustment he had made on the large tree butt. The stand broke out and he slid down the tree, hugging it all the way. Had he picked a tree with more uniform diameter, he would not have encountered difficulty.

Another factor to consider is your background. Walk around and look where deer are likely to appear, then look at where you will be in the tree. Will you stick out against the sky like a sore thumb, or will you blend in with green, brown, or gray vegetation in the background? I prefer hunting from trees that have some foliage to hide me, but without limbs and branches that block my shot.

When selecting a tree, it is wise to bring your stand so you can put it up into the tree. Take a small hand axe or saw for trimming branches. Study the position you will be in on opening day. Can you move in the direction you like? Can you see as much as you like? Take your time; choosing the right tree can be critical to your success or failure.

Many hunters wait until the morning of the hunt to try out a new tree stand. Some even carry their stands in the original packing cartons, then are shocked to find they have to assemble the stand. Many stands require 30 to 40 minutes to assemble. It is better to put it together at home. Be sure to take all of the squeaks and other noises out of the stand. Practice putting it up in a tree in your backyard or at a nearby woods. Learn how to safely take your firearm up into the stand without damaging the gun. This practice will give you the confidence necessary to be a successful hunter.

One of my favorite stands is a large climbing tree stand that I painted gray. I've killed several deer from this stand, which blends in well in the heavy pine forest where I do a lot of my hunting.

**Carry a Day Pack**

Always carry a day pack (page 143) with enough essentials so you can stay a full day on the tree stand. The majority of large bucks are taken between 9 a.m. and 3 p.m. Many stand hunters become bored, tired, cold, or impatient about mid-morning, then leave their stands to stretch their muscles, or to head back to camp or their vehicles. They don't return to their tree stands until late afternoon, then hunt until dark.

The hunter with a day pack loaded with provisions can remain on the stand all day. This gives him an opportunity to spot those large bucks that tend to move when many hunters are absent from the woods.

In your day pack, carry such items as food, hot drink, a first-aid kit, empty containers for urination to save trips down the tree, extra clothing and ammunition, and survival gear. There are many other items, depending on the needs of each hunter, that can be carried. You can attach the day pack to your tree stand and carry it up as you climb, or tie it to a rope and lift it up into the tree along with your gun or bow.

*By carrying provisions in a day pack, this hunter can remain on his stand all day.*

### Use Binoculars

Another important item is binoculars. With my binoculars, I have spotted many deer that, in years gone by, I would have overlooked. Binoculars can be especially helpful during the rifle season. A tree stand that has been properly placed may provide shots up to 200 yards.

### Other Equipment

A camouflage face mask, such as the type used by turkey hunters, is also a good idea. I have heard many hunters say that when deer looked at them, the animals always stared into their eyes. What these hunters failed to recognize is that their white faces, not eyes, were the most visible parts of their bodies. A camouflage mask will make you less visible, but not restrict your vision. White hands can also give away the hunter; camouflage gloves will correct that problem.

Many stand hunters wear snowmobile suits and insulated boots. They keep their clothing loose, so it does not restrict circulation to their hands and feet. Much of their clothing is wool and they wear such things as Balaclava-type hats, which are extremely warm and may be worn either as a hat or rolled down to cover the face and neck, much like a ski mask.

Be sure to bring along several elastic shock cords of varying lengths. Shock cords with an S-hook on each end can be used to hang such things as your coat, day pack, lunch, or whatever. Use the shock cord to secure the hand climber portion of the tree stand so it is out of the way. You certainly don't want the hand climber to fall at a critical moment.

Many stand hunters like to use rangefinders, such as those made by the Ranging Corporation. They enable hunters to determine distances out to where the target is likely to appear.

Perhaps the most important item is a safety belt. Not only does it keep you from falling, it will also help to steady your aim, especially when shooting a rifle or muzzleloader at deer some distance away. A properly-adjusted safety belt can make the entire day go a lot smoother, because it eliminates the fear of falling. Each year, several hunters are killed from falling or having

*For safety and convenience, use a rope to lift your bow and arrows or rifle into the stand.*

their firearms discharge while climbing into their stands.

Before going to your stand each morning, put on a scent to cover up your smell. There are many scents on the market, all of which can mask your odor.

Since a buck has his nose tuned in at all times for unfamiliar odors, the stand hunter would be wise to avoid smoking and packing strong-smelling food in his lunch. Along the same lines, if nature calls, leave your stand and travel a good distance downwind before answering the call. Or use a bottle that can be tightly capped. Keep your stand area as odor-free as possible.

**Be Alert & Patient**

When you arrive at your stand site on opening morning, first check the wind. Select the stand that is downwind from your watching area. Get comfortable before daylight. As the new day dawns, be still and alert. Remember that as long as a deer doesn't smell you or see you move, he will follow his usual routine. Use your ears and listen for any sounds that might reveal the presence of deer.

It bears repeating that the stand hunter must be patient. Don't give up just because you failed to see a deer on your first day. If you researched your stand site and if you found ample sign, then you are probably in a good area. Maybe the deer fed during the night or maybe the sudden influx of hunters caused them to stay bedded. Remain on your stand for at least three days before you consider changing locations.

The stand hunter who penetrates the backcountry, thinks like a deer, is patient and watches the wind, will probably enjoy venison every year of his hunting career.

# 7

# Scrape Hunting
# for Trophy Bucks

A fter sitting in a cold tree stand for a whole morning watching two scraped-out spots on an old logging road 30 yards away, I felt I might be the victim of a practical joke. I certainly had never heard of hunting whitetail bucks in such a fashion.

As time passed, I started daydreaming about the events that led me here. I had recently moved to south Georgia to run a wild-life management program for the University of Georgia. When deer season opened, I took off a few days to try my hand at killing a buck in the flat, pine-palmetto woods west of the Okefenokee Swamp. I had enjoyed many successful deer hunts in the Appalachian Mountains, so I thought the same hunting methods would work down here. How wrong could I be! After several days without even seeing a deer, I was ready to give up. The habits of the southern, flat-woods whitetails had me totally confused.

J. Lee Rentz, then manager of the Suwannoochee Wildlife Management Area, recognized that I was having trouble hunting this swampy terrain. "Get into my truck," he told me. "I'm going to teach you how to hunt deer." I knew he had spent many years working with whitetails, so I welcomed the opportunity.

"The most predictable thing we know about whitetail bucks is that they are unpredictable," J. Lee began. "I only know of one thing that bucks do consistently enough for hunters to rely on, and that's work scrapes. I'm sure they didn't teach you college boys about scrapes in school, but no matter where you find whitetail bucks, they work scrapes. Scrape hunting will get you a good trophy."

We continued riding until we came to the edge of a recent clear-cut. Leaving the truck, we started walking along the edge, where the clear-cut and the adjacent woods met. We immediately started finding fresh rubs on small saplings growing next to the woods. Suddenly J. Lee stopped. Pointing at a scraped-out spot about two feet in diameter, he told me to pick up a handful of the sandy soil and smell it. Stooping down, I grabbed some of the dirt; it had the strong smell of urine.

"Now look up," he instructed.

I did, and saw where the overhanging bushes were broken and shredded about four feet above the scrape.

"This is a sure sign of a mature buck," J. Lee continued. "If

*Most scrapes are made by bucks 2½ years or older. This young whitetail is visiting another buck's scrape.*

you follow the edge of this clear-cut, you will probably find several more scrapes. When a buck is in the peak of his rut, he will stake out his territory by arbitrarily making scrapes. Then, he will check his scrapes, number one, to see if an interested doe has been by, and number two, to see if another buck has entered his territory."

"How will he know?"

"The visiting deer will usually paw the scrape and urinate on it," J. Lee responded. "If there isn't a doe hanging around or a rival buck spoiling for a fight, the home buck will freshen his scrape by urinating in it and chewing the overhanging branches. Also, he will probably rub his antlers on nearby saplings. Now, all you have to do is sprinkle a few drops of urine-based deer lure in the scrape, then move to one side where the wind won't blow your scent to the scrape. Find a good hiding spot and wait for old mossy horns to stagger in. He will be somewhat careless because he's love-sick. Remember when you were sixteen? Now get out there and find some fresh scrapes. These bucks are at the peak of their rut and there are plenty of fresh scrapes to be found."

Suddenly I was startled from daydreaming by a grunting sound coming from the logging road. Since there were wild hogs in the area, I was sure it was an old boar coming to root around in my carefully-selected scrape. I caught a movement off to my right, and slowly turning, saw a six-point buck boldly walking down the road. He was heading for the scrape—I couldn't believe it! This buck was breaking all the rules. He was moving during the middle of the day, he wasn't using any caution, and he wasn't being quiet. He approached the scrape stiff-legged with his nose held high. As I eased my .30-06 into shooting position, I knew I was not the victim of a joke, but rather the very fortunate student of a dependable way to hunt whitetails.

The following year I was bowhunting off the coast of Georgia on Blackbeard Island. Not being familiar with the island, I spent the first day scouting. On the south end I found several scrapes in a thicket between two large sand dunes. The scrapes were freshly pawed and the dirt smelled like a courthouse restroom.

Early the next morning, I sprinkled deer lure on my boots and slipped into the thicket to squirt lure on each of the three scrapes. Then I selected a tree some 25 yards downwind for my portable tree stand. I waited all day. Late that afternoon, I heard a noise that sounded like a wounded elephant coming through the thicket. It was a nice eight-point buck. He was grunting, pawing, and thrashing the bushes with his antlers. Three arrows later, his tail waved good-bye as he bounded, unharmed, over a sand dune. I didn't take home any venison, but I had become a firm believer in scrape hunting.

Many years have passed since my introduction to scrape hunting. I have spent each season since trying to perfect this method of hunting. Fortunately, I've received some expert help along the way. Some of the most interesting information was provided by Francis X. Lueth, one of the nation's foremost whitetail biologists. Francis has worked with white-tailed deer for almost 40 years. He retired from the Alabama Game and Fish Division after 30 years of whitetail research to become a deer management consultant.

When asked about whitetail scrapes, he quickly pointed out that he was giving me only his opinion based on his observations and research. Different biologists have different opinions about this phenomenon.

For someone to be a good scrape hunter, Francis began, he should understand the rut. The rut, he said, is an evolutionary thing that has been worked out over hundreds of years so fawns will be weaned at the same time the mast falls. Because of

*Ben Rodgers Lee, the author, and Fred Bear study a fresh deer rub on a small sapling.*

this and several other reasons, the rut varies from area to area in any given state.

The hunter should also know something about rubs. There are two kinds. The first, which occurs during late summer or early fall, is by bucks rubbing velvet off their new antlers. The second type is during the peak of the rut, at the same time bucks are making scrapes. These rubs are probably used to mark the buck's territory. Apparently the buck leaves his scent by rubbing a gland found near the eye.

Scrapes are made mostly by dominant bucks that are 2½ years or older. This is just what the trophy hunter likes to hear! Most scrapes are made on the fringes of the buck's territory, and more often than not, will be at the base of a bush.

I asked Francis if a buck had a set number of scrapes or if they have any particular configuration. The answer was no, to both questions. "Sometimes you may find several in a row along a logging road, and again, you may find only one or two on a ridge. But there is no known pattern."

The buck works his scrapes for periods of up to 30 days. However, this may vary, depending on the availability of does, man's intrusion, etc.

To learn more about scrape hunting and to obtain more opinions from wildlife biologists, I surveyed 36 wildlife agencies throughout the whitetail range. I obtained answers from Saskatchewan to Florida, receiving a variety of responses to the following:

1) The dates of their whitetail seasons; 2) estimated date of the peak of the rut; 3) did the rutting dates vary in their area, and if so, why; 4) were scrapes made by rutting bucks; 5) did anyone hunt scrapes; and 6) in their opinion, does it pay to hunt scrapes.

The results were interesting. The peak of the rut in most areas occurred during November (in many states, it peaked during the archery season). In almost half of the states, the rutting period varied throughout the state. As to why the rutting date varied, the biologists were not consistent in their opinions. Many indicated temperature changes, hormonal activity triggered by varying sunlight, heredity, diet, and north-south latitude variation. Many said the peak varied from year to year in the same region, because of changes in population, available food, weather, etc. Almost all of the biologists agreed that whitetail bucks made scrapes. Two replies from the Plains States questioned how

*At scrapes, whitetails also leave their scent by chewing a branch directly above the pawed-out dirt.*

much scrape hunting was actually done in their states. Most said there was little scrape hunting in their area and eight said they knew of no one who used the technique.

Perhaps the most important information obtained from the survey were the results from the last question: "Do you think scrape hunting would pay off in your area?" Only three biologists said no, and again these people were from Plains States. But 28 of the biologists replied with a firm yes, while five indicated yes under varying circumstances. The survey left little doubt that throughout most of the whitetail range, scrape hunting is a technique that will work, though it is still new to most hunters.

**How to Scrape Hunt**

The actual scrape hunting technique is quite simple. Let's take it from the top.

1) During the summer, select your hunting area. Locate a biologist who is either responsible for that area or familiar with it. Ask him the probable date of the rut and when it will peak. This will be the best time to hunt scrapes.

2) Once you know when the rut is likely to occur, find out

which type of hunting is allowed during that period. You may have to pick up your bow or muzzleloader to hunt during the rut.

3)   While waiting for the hunting season, find a source of buck lure made up primarily of urine. Your sporting goods dealer can help you. Many dedicated scrape hunters collect urine from the bladder of their deer, put it in a tightly-sealed plastic bottle, and use it the following year.

4)   As the rutting season approaches, begin to scout your hunting area. Look for rubs on saplings or small trees, and for scrapes. Don't let earlier rubs fool you. The early rubs are usually in more secluded thickets and will be obviously old. Try to find rubs that are fresh and in more open areas, often near or at scrapes. As for the latter, watch for them along logging roads, at the edges of fields, and if you live in hilly or mountainous country, in high places where the vegetation is not too thick. Avoid getting excited over bird scratchings, especially wild turkey. The scrape itself may be as small as a magazine or as large as a dining room table.

*Muzzleloader deer hunter studies a scrape along an old logging road.*

5)   Determine that the scrape is fresh. Has the dirt been disturbed recently? Does the soil have a strong urine odor? Have the overhanging bushes been chewed? Are there fresh rubs in the area? If the answer to these questions is yes, you are on a hot one! Be cautious. Leave as little human scent as possible. Try putting urine deer lure on your boots and trouser cuffs to cover up your scent.

6)   Check out the surrounding area for more scrapes. In the case of a field edge, logging road, or ridgetop, walk along the feature for several hundred yards. The ideal setup is to get where you can see several scrapes from one position. More than once I have seen bucks' territories overlap, with each animal having scrapes in the same area. If you find one of these places, you're all set for the hunt of a lifetime.

7)   Once you have found a group of scrapes, select several possible blinds, because in the morning, the wind may be blowing in a different direction. Make sure you can see all around each scrape. Nothing is more frustrating than to be in a fallen treetop watching a scrape and when the buck arrives, find that branches prevent you from seeing more than its hind quarter.

8)   On the day of the hunt, squirt a few drops of deer lure in the scrape. Then soak a small piece of flannel cloth in urine deer lure and hang it on a bush near a fresh scrape. The cloth should be about five feet off the ground. Take a well-hidden stand downwind.

9)   Arrive before daylight and stay until dark. Remain observant throughout the day. Remember, a buck in rut feeds very little and breaks the early-morning, late-afternoon movement patterns. He is likely to show up at any time. Also listen for any unusual sounds. You may hear a buck before you see him.

10)   Plan on spending at least three days watching the scrapes.

As with most techniques, scrape hunting demands patience and alertness, but when you know there is a buck in the area and that he'll be back, patience is a lot easier to come by. In scrape hunting, you have that knowledge.

# 8

# The Solo Hunter

The night before opening morning of the deer season, he cannot sleep. It is almost as though the night were eternal. As he tosses and turns, he thinks back on the hours at the rifle range, working with the old '06 so it will shoot true with every shot. He relives the scouting trips, and in his fitful attempt to find sleep, vividly pictures the white oak flat, with all its deer signs, where dawn will find him.

As he finally slips into a deep sleep, there is a satisfied feeling within him. Tomorrow, he will spend the day silently, alone, hunting the whitetail buck. It will be a challenging day afield, man against trophy, one on one. And whether he scores or the buck outwits him, it will be a successful, memorable hunt, because he is a *solo hunter.*

I have come to regard the stand and stalk hunters as solo hunters because their sport, as opposed to hunting with dogs or drives with two or more hunters, involves only one man, unaided. I am a solo hunter, and it has given me many years of fun and excitement, plus I have had the good fortune of bagging a fair number of whitetails.

Solo hunters are probably the most successful at taking deer. This is not to say that I oppose deer drives and hunting with dogs. Far from it. I have participated in both types of hunting and enjoyed my outings. Some of my best friends are deeply involved in both; but for me, I like my woods quiet. I can live without the sound of warhoops, hunting by somebody else's rules, barking dogs, and lots of people scattered about.

Whether he uses a bow, muzzleloading rifle, or modern firearm, the solo hunter must spend many hours on the range getting in tune. He practices hard for that one, all-important shot which, in all likelihood, will either put meat on the table or cause many excuses around the campfire.

If the solo hunter is worth his salt, he has done a thorough job of scouting. He knows the location of deer, what they are eating, the approximate date of the rut, and which trails they are using. He is not entering the woods hoping that a deer will blunder past his stand. With the knowledge that comes with pre-season scouting, he can place a tree stand downwind from a trail or a set of scrapes. He can erect a ground blind in a white oak grove or along the edge of an oat field.

The solo hunter depends on his own skills to find and outsmart a buck. He devotes many hours to studying the habits and habitat of his quarry. He learns how to read sign and the ever-changing movement patterns of whitetails. He knows how to make allies of adversaries, like the wind, rain, temperature changes, the moon, and actions of other hunters. His training includes field courses in patience, sharp eyesight, keen hearing, and moving as slowly and silently as the fog. And, he's in good enough physical condition to walk all day.

All this may sound as if solo hunting demands mastering complicated skills; don't be misled, it does not. It is one of the most enjoyable and productive methods left to us by our ancestors.

I have heard literally hundreds of hunting tales, but I still enjoy listening to a solo hunter who has spent the day on a tree stand. He has had the privilege of watching nature for one full day, uninterrupted by man. I know men who hunt from a stand and each day, become as excited as kids at a birthday party as they relive their experiences. They see a bobcat trying to ambush a wild turkey, a raccoon chasing a crawfish, or a squirrel gathering acorns for its winter food cache. This same patient hunter will sit near a buck's scrape and in all probability, stride back into camp with that grin that says there will be fresh meat for the Dutch oven.

For me, the greatest thrill of each deer season is to spend a few days stalk hunting on private property, where there are no

*To get her trophy whitetail, this solo hunter spent an entire day concealed in a cold ground stand.*

**The author glasses a distant field while solo hunting for whitetails.**

other hunters. To move through the forest like a shadow, without interference, is an experience I look forward to each autumn.

Many times I have tried to analyze why this method stands above all others. Perhaps it's the challenge of outsmarting a deer or perhaps the opportunity to prove to myself that I'm as good an outdoorsman as I think I am. Then again, deep in my mind, perhaps I see myself 200 years ago in the heart of Cherokee country. Whatever the reason, the experience is the kind that makes a man glad to be alive and part of the natural scheme of things.

My stalk hunts have provided many of my favorite memories. I can recall a stalk in the mountains near Tellico Plains, Tennessee, where I watched a parade of bucks, nose to tail and far out of range, move across the skyline late one afternoon. And, there's the hunt many years ago in the Choccolocco Management Area in Alabama, which resulted in a beautiful nine-point buck taken on a beech flat splashed with fall colors.

There was another memorable hunt in Greene County,

*Hundreds of hours of practice culminated in one well-placed shot and an unforgettable trophy for this Wisconsin bow hunter.*

Georgia, when I walked right up to three does bedded under a cedar during a cold, driving downpour. While not nearly all my hunts produce deer, they are successful in that I can immerse myself in an outdoor setting that most modern men don't even know exists.

As a stalk hunter, I can ease along logging roads, quietly observing feeding areas or move from shadow to shadow, watching and listening for the sounds that might give away a deer's whereabouts. And when the moment of truth comes, I will have a clear shot at an animal that is not spooked, making my one-shot kill much easier.

To me, solo hunting is a lifelong quest to learn new hunting skills and improve old ones. It is a never-ending search for more information about the animal and its surroundings.

It is, I believe, our duty to keep this fine old art alive. Solo hunting is a great way to introduce youngsters to the world of hunting. Granted, they will want to talk, step on sticks, and move too fast at first, but after a few trips, the young hunters will begin to change. They, too, will start to realize that solo hunting is much more than taking a deer along the side of a road. It is an annual reunion with nature—precious moments and new learning experiences that will last a lifetime in memories. And because of it, you will become a richer person in mind and spirit. I guarantee it.

# 9

# Deer Drives That Work

A cold, ten-mile-per-hour wind had blown out of the north all morning. At noon, my two companions and I met back at the car and exchanged hunting reports. No one had seen a deer. It was one of those days when whitetails refuse to move.

As we ate lunch and discussed the merits of going home to do some reloading, I kept looking at a topo map of the area. There was a narrow, deep creek bottom that interested me. Having scouted the area thoroughly before deer season, I remembered that the creek bottom was thick with low-growing vines, cane, and other vegetation—a great place for an old buck to hole up during foul weather.

It was worth a try. "Gentlemen," I announced, "we are going to brave the weather one more time and put on a three-man drive." Although they expressed some doubts, my friends agreed to give it a try. Since it was my idea, I would go up to the head of the creek bottom and fight the thick brush, gradually moving down through the area. Meanwhile, they would each take a stand along high, steep ridges overlooking the bottom. The topo map made planning the drive easy.

By 1 p.m., we were in position and I began picking my way noisily down the draw. At times I had to wade the icy water; other times I didn't think I could squeeze through the dense stands of cane. Stopping to adjust my blaze-orange vest, I began to question my decision. Then I heard the crack of a rifle. My spirits were lifted and I started to fight the brush with renewed energy. As I neared the point where my companions had taken stands, a second blast sounded.

Shortly, I emerged from the bottom and started looking for my cohorts. I found one of them partly up the steep ridge, busily field-dressing a seven-point buck. Then the second stander walked up, mumbling something about his scope being off. He had missed a huge buck.

As we helped field-dress the buck, we all agreed that the short drive had turned a day not fittin' for deer hunting into an afternoon with fast action and success. We had seen proof that deer drives will work.

Driving is a method of hunting whereby walking hunters or dogs push deer toward hunters on stands. Dog drives are conducted in thick cover in the Deep South. They require lots of hunters and usually produce quick running shots that require a shotgun and buckshot. Because this type of hunting is not permitted in most states, we will not dwell on the technique.

On the other hand, slow-moving, hunters-only deer drives have a place in many areas. In most situations, driving for deer is saved for last, after other methods have failed. In Wisconsin, for example, hunters tend to avoid drives during the first weekend

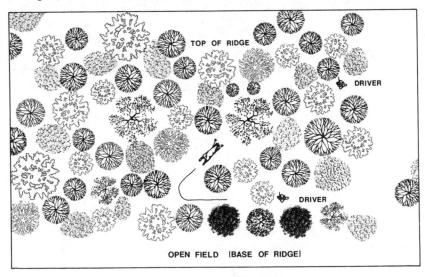

**Two-Man Ridge Drive**

*Experienced hunters look for deer sign, then plan a drive that takes into account deer movements along with feeding and bedding areas.*

of the gun season, and then switch to drives after that. However, some hunters prefer driving over all other types of hunting.

The number of hunters required to conduct a drive depends on the terrain and cover. A large wooded tract with no natural barriers such as rivers or ravines may require as many as 30 hunters, with one-third of them serving as *posters,* or *standers,* and the rest as *drivers.* On the other hand, three hunters can make a drive in a narrow valley or a small block of woods surrounded by open terrain.

Many hunters like to make noisy drives. The drivers shout, beat pots and pans tied to their belts, or make any noise they can. These hunters believe that spooked, hard-running deer are less cautious, so the posters have a better chance of seeing the fleeing animals.

Other drivers prefer to move quietly and slowly, hoping to ease deer out in front of them.

**Large Group Drives**

In a group drive, the drivers move downwind toward standers that overlook good shooting lands such as logging roads, fields, powerline corridors, and fire lanes. These drives require more planning and coordination, simply because more hunters are involved.

The density of the cover determines the distance between drivers. They should be close enough so a buck will not slip between them and escape to the rear. Another trick of older bucks is to stay bedded in thick cover and let the drivers pass. After the hunters walk by, they slip away. As the line of drivers start toward the standers, the two edge drivers should move slightly ahead of the others. This prevents a buck from sneaking around the edge of the line.

### Small Group Drives

On many days, small group drives are much more effective than other methods of hunting. Following are some of the conditions under which hunters should consider such a drive:

*Weather.* There are days when deer bed down and move as little as possible. I have seen deer stay bedded with almost no movement for as long as five days. Strong winds, snowstorms, heavy rains, unseasonably hot weather—all are conditions that cause deer to remain in their beds.

*Feeding Habits.* Deer will often change their feeding habits, eating almost exclusively at night and moving little during the day. It has been my experience that whitetails often feed on bright nights, such as during a full moon or when there is a good ground cover of snow. When deer are night-feeding, stand or stalk hunting may be less productive.

*Hunting Pressure.* Many times, especially in areas with a long hunting season, I have heard hunters complain that all the deer have been pushed out of their area. The truth is, in areas with a lot of hunting pressure, whitetails become quickly conditioned to moving at night rather than during the day. This is especially true of older bucks. Heavy hunting pressure may also cause deer to bunch up in swamps, remote corners, thick creek or river bottoms, and other areas overlooked by hunters. Such places afford an excellent opportunity for a small group drive.

*Other Pressures.* Other factors may cause deer to become nocturnal in their feeding habits. These include timber-cutting operations, controlled burns, road construction, farming, free-ranging dogs, and even snowmobiling. In these situations, driving may be the only way to bag a buck in thick cover.

*Terrain.* Steep, narrow ravines and canyons with thick cover in the bottom are perfect places to drive. Posters should pay special attention to the smaller ravines that descend into the main corridor. Deer moving ahead of the driver usually try to slip out through these brushy cuts. Small bogs or marshes clogged with brush are commonly driven by hunters in northern states.

## How to Conduct a Drive

The first step in making a successful drive is to scout the area carefully. Study a topo map until you have a good picture of the terrain. Be sure to bring your map on scouting trips. Mark the places where you find deer sign, so you can plan your hunt more carefully.

As you scout the area, be sure to note places where you can conduct drives. Islands of cover are ideal, such as a narrow strip of woods with a clear-cut on one side and a road on the other. Look for any tract of woods or brush fringed by open areas.

Small group drives are as varied in design as the terrain. However, the following basic methods are good examples of how drives should be designed.

*Logging Road Drive.* Two friends use this drive effectively in areas with a lot of logging roads. They select a road that runs parallel to a thick area, like a creek bottom, cane thicket, swamp, or older clear-cut. One of the hunters eases down the road at a very

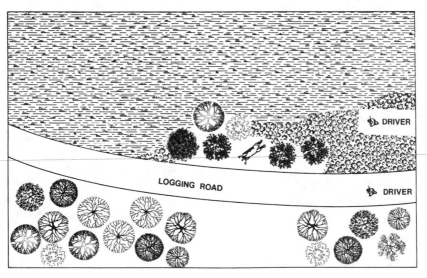

**Logging Road Drive**

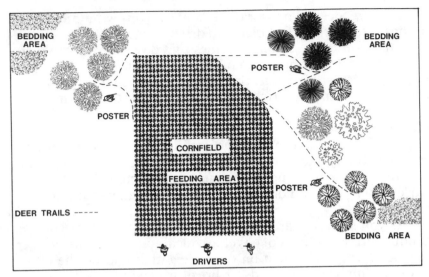

**Deer Trail Drive**

slow pace, while the other walks parallel to the road, moving as quietly as possible through the thick cover. He tries to remain about 50 to 100 yards from the road. The hunters try to stay abreast of one another. A whitetail flushed by the hunter in cover usually gets up well ahead and is seldom spooked. It trots out to the logging road, then stops to see what was moving in the cover. At that point, the hunter in the road gets a good shot.

*Deer Trail Drive.* This drive, which takes advantage of the natural movements of deer, is more complicated and requires a great deal of scouting. It also requires a working knowledge of the terrain, deer habits, and movements. While scouting, hunters must pinpoint feeding and bedding areas, and trails connecting these areas.

Conduct the drive at daybreak. Posters should take their stands on trails leading from the feeding areas to bedding spots. The drivers then move slowly and quietly through the feeding grounds. Once they detect the approaching drivers, deer move along the trails to hide in their bedding areas. This type of drive can be conducted by a small group of hunters. It is one of the best drives for hunters with muzzleloaders or bows, because most shots are at close range.

*Two-man Ridge Drive.* This drive dates back to the 1700s when the longhunters roamed the Appalachian Mountains. It is

*Fears moves slowly and quietly while making a logging road drive with a companion (not visible in photo). He keeps his eyes glued on the cover, where his partner is likely to push out deer.*

conducted by two hunters moving along the side of a ridge or mountain. One walks along the lower part and the other moves parallel, but just below the top of the ridge and a few yards behind the other hunter. The lower hunter jumps bucks lying along flats and benches on the side of the ridge. To escape, the deer usually circle up and back along the ridge where the other hunter gets a shot.

Planning is one of the most important elements in any drive. Each member of the drive should be fully aware of the entire plan and his role. A well-executed drive is like a well-executed football play—each member of the team must do his part right.

Before everyone heads into the woods, review your plans on the topo map. Set times for the drive to begin and end. Years ago, I was part of a deer drive in Colorado where my guide did not set a time or place to meet once the drive was over. For most of our party, the drive ended at four that afternoon. But we didn't find two of the standers until long after dark. Such poorly-planned drives are seldom successful.

Safety should be on the mind of every hunter in a deer drive. This is another reason why everyone should understand every facet of the drive. Each driver must wear blaze orange. Posters must be certain of their target. It is also a good idea for posters to take elevated stands so their shots angle downward into the ground. Drivers must be careful about taking long-range shots.

Each poster should remain on his stand until the drive is over. I try to make it a point to drive only with individuals who I know to be safe hunters.

# 10

# Rattling

Outside of Texas, the least understood method of hunting whitetail bucks is *rattling*. The technique was developed and gradually refined in Texas and is now spreading throughout the whitetail range.

Rattling simply involves banging together a pair of deer antlers to imitate a fight between two bucks. Done during the rut, it attracts bucks for two reasons. First, the buck whose territory you have invaded will come running to find out who has ventured into his domain. The second reason is that younger, less dominant bucks will ease up to a fight between dominant bucks and try to steal any does that might be watching.

For rattling to be successful, you have to be in an area with a ratio of one buck for every two does, or less. If the ratio is greater, say one buck for four does, there are plenty of does to go around and such amorous activities as fighting or stealing does is uncommon and unnecessary. Before you make plans to try rattling, call a game biologist responsible for your hunting area and get his opinion as to the buck-doe ratio.

Because rattling works only during the rut, you would be wise to find out when the rut peaks in your area. Assuming the season is open during that time, plan your hunt for the week before or the week after the rut peaks. Bucks will be more prone to investigate your rattling during this period.

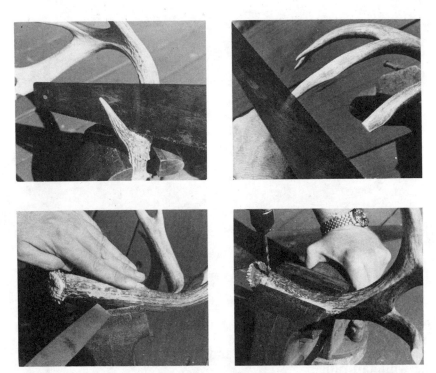

*Steps for making a set of rattling antlers include (clockwise from top-left): Saw off the brow tine, then cut one inch from the tip of each point; smooth the area where you will hold the antler, then drill a hole so you can attach a carrying cord.*

*Following the steps above will produce a finished pair of rattling "horns."*

Rattling requires a special piece of equipment—a set of fairly large (at least three points per side) antlers. Here is how you can make your own:

1) Secure a set of antlers. It may be antlers you found in the woods or a pair sawed off a buck you killed. Sometimes meat processors have sets that go unclaimed by hunters. Taxidermists are also a good source.

2) Put the antlers in a vice and saw off the brow tine, or guard point.

3) Next, saw off about one inch from the tip of each tine. This protects your hands when rattling and provides a better sound at long distances.

4) Using a file, smooth the area where you sawed off the brow tine. Since this is where you hold the antlers, it will make rattling more comfortable.

5) Drill a hole through the base of the antlers, so you can attach a carrying cord.

6) Tie the antlers on each end of a two-foot section of strong, dark-colored cord. This makes it easier to carry the antlers and keeps you from losing one of the pair.

7) Paint the antlers fluorescent orange, an important step in hunter safety.

**Choose A Site**

Your next move is to scout out two or three sites in which to rattle up a buck. It is important to find an area that has fresh rubs and scrapes. Once again, mark them on your topo map so you can return to the spot on opening morning.

The best conditions for rattling up a buck include a cold, clear day with little or no wind. The sound of your rattling will travel clearly in all directions, which is important because you don't know where bucks are located.

On the morning of your hunt, sprinkle plenty of buck lure on your hunting coat and trousers. It will cover your scent and help to excite the bucks.

Select a stand downwind from an active scrape. Be sure that your cover is open enough for you to see in all directions. Many bucks, especially the less dominant ones or those not fully in rut, will often circle the sound of a fight, so you must have clear visibility all around your stand. The dominant buck will most likely come running, often right up to you. And remember, remain at your stand even during midday hours, because bucks in the rut move about anytime during the day.

**How to Rattle**
  1)    Grip each antler firmly at the base. The tines of the two antlers should point toward each other.
  2)    Bang the antler in the right hand hard against the antler in your left hand; make sure the tines strike each other.
  3)    While the antlers are interlocked, twist your wrist hard to make the tines rattle against one another. Continue this noise for ten seconds, then jerk the antlers apart sharply.
  4)    Use the antlers to scrape the soil, leaves, sticks, rocks, or whatever is on the ground. Be as loud as you can.
  5)    Reach over and beat the antlers against the bushes around your stand. It should sound like a buck fight, so make it last for up to one minute.
  6)    Pause for a minute, then rattle the antlers for five seconds. Stop for another minute.
  7)    Next, rattle the tips of the tines together for five seconds. Stop for two to three minutes.

*Rattling brought this buck within easy range.*

*Author Fears rattling for whitetails. The technique works best either the week before or after the peak of the rut.*

8)    Scrape the ground and leaves five or six times. Stop for two minutes.

9)    Sharply strike one of the antler bases on the ground three times.

This is the basic rattling routine. After completing the procedure, wait five minutes and then repeat, but make it a little quieter than the first. Go through at least five routines before you give up and move to another location.

When rattling, keep your bow or rifle handy, because a buck may run in at any moment. When not rattling, watch and listen.

Bucks in the rut are less wary and spoiling for a fight, so they often come right up to a rattling hunter. This gives you enough time to size up his rack and to pick your shot.

A buck called in by rattling is excited and his adrenaline is flowing. For this reason, you should be shooting a heavier load than normal. An excited buck can take a hard hit and still manage to get away.

A word of caution about rattling in a heavily-hunted forest: hunters, like bucks, get excited when they hear what they think are bucks fighting. Do not rattle where you might be putting yourself in danger. Rattle only on private property, on leased hunting lands, or where you are sure that you won't rattle up a careless hunter. Be sure to wear hunter-orange clothing, especially on the upper half of your body.

At the end of the season, give your rattling antlers a good soaking in linseed oil to prevent dry rot. Also, practice rattling before the next season opens. Under the right conditions, a hunter who knows how to rattle will be the envy at the meat pole and taxidermist.

# 11

# Deer Hunting
# After Opening Day

One of the most frustrating events in a deer hunter's life is missing opening day. Most believe, and with good reason, it is the best time of the entire season. Deer are not as wary and they go about their daily routines as usual. After opening day, however, they change their patterns quickly. The woods are alive with hunters, strange scents are everywhere, shots are being fired, and traffic on logging roads is heavy. All this activity makes deer much more cautious—they move less during the day and more at night.

If you missed opening morning, don't give up deer hunting. There are techniques that you can still use to get your buck, even when the hunting pressure is heavy. To understand why these methods are effective, we must first know how most bucks react to hunting pressure.

Deer, unlike people, don't reason; their behavior is a learned reaction to what's going on around them. The sudden influx of strange and frightening sounds, smells, and sights cause them to change their daily behavior. Older bucks, especially, become conditioned to move when man-related activities are at a minimum, such as midday or night. They seek out pockets in the woods that hunters overlook or those that are so thick and/or inaccessible that hunters avoid them. In short, whitetails do everything they can to avoid man; if the pressure becomes too great, they will change their habits drastically. Let's see how we can use this fact to our advantage.

When hunting in areas with heavy pressure, one of the best times to pursue whitetails is midday. Even in public hunting areas, most hunters are afield from sunrise to 9 or 10 a.m., then return to their camps or vehicles to wait until mid-afternoon, when they head back into the woods. Deer, and especially bucks, are quick to pick up on the reduced activity. On public areas, I have often seen more deer during midday than I normally observed early and late. For several years, I managed a private hunting lodge in which the policy was to put out the hunters before daylight and pick them up at 10 a.m. The hunters ate a leisurely lunch in the lodge and were not taken back out again until 2 p.m. or later.

While I worked at the lodge, anytime I wanted to get pictures of big bucks, I would go out after the hunters were brought in, get in a blind, and would soon be photographing deer. It amazed me how quickly these animals learned that the hunting pressure was off during midday. By taking a day pack and hunting all day long, you may also find that the most productive hours are in the middle of the day.

A second consideration is to seek out locations that are usually overlooked by most hunters. In seasons past I have been surprised at the number of bucks that remained around our lodge. In fact, one of the largest bucks stayed within 100 yards of where we butcher our deer. Since all of my hunting guests wanted to hunt in remote areas, the bucks reacted to the pressure by moving into thick pockets of brush near our facilities.

At another lodge that I managed for several years, some of the best hunting was in a narrow strip of woods between a major U.S. highway and a large clear-cut. None of the hunters considered it a good place to hunt and rarely did anyone go near the strip of woods. But when my biologists checked it out, they found several large bucks.

At one public hunting area where I worked, the best bucks would always spend the hunting season around the checking station, because no one ever hunted the area.

Take a hard look at the entire area in which you plan to hunt. If you expect heavy hunting pressure, check out little pockets of cover that other hunters might overlook. Also, look for any facilities where hunters would not feel like they are in a wilderness setting. Other places to consider are areas with extremely thick

*Swamps, creek bottoms, and dense thickets are ideal hangouts for bucks during periods of intense hunting pressure.*

cover, such as creek bottoms, river banks, or swamps. Older bucks, in particular, seek out these spots during heavy hunting pressure. Many bed down in the dense thickets during daylight hours, then feed under the cover of darkness.

If you hunt from a portable tree stand, look for one of these thickets, then position your stand so you can look down into it. Spend the entire day observing the area. Granted, you will probably see fewer deer than hunters who overlook vast, open areas, but when you do see a whitetail, it will generally be a good-sized buck.

### Use a Canoe

Large swamps can be difficult to hunt, but often hold deer. Many contain little islands scattered throughout the wetland. My favorite way to hunt these remote islands, as well as rivers and streams, is by canoe. You can move silently in a canoe, reducing the chance of spooking whitetails.

State hunting laws will dictate how you can use your canoe for hunting. In some states, you are not permitted to shoot from a canoe; in others, only if game is out of the water. Check first, before you make plans.

If you cannot shoot from a canoe, use it as a means of getting into unhunted areas, then stalk hunt or drive the low areas as conditions dictate.

When hunting from a canoe, use cover scent, keep the wind in your favor, blend in with the surroundings as much as safe hunting will permit, and keep noise and motion to a minimum. Hunt from a canoe much like you would stalk hunt on foot. But now you are simply stalking along the water's edge.

I currently use a camouflage canoe made by Mad River Canoe Company in Vermont. I find it amazing that I am seeing more deer from this canoe, which seems to melt into the vegetation along the backwaters.

Using a canoe for hunting is not something you should tackle for the first time during deer season. Before you hunt, learn canoeing skills during the summer. Get to know the backwaters, river, creek, or marsh before the hunting season. Take all necessary safety precautions.

Hunting after opening day is a challenge, especially for those who hunt public hunting areas. By studying the situation and knowing something about deer when the pressure is on, your outing can be more interesting and rewarding than if you hunted on opening morning.

*Some manufacturers make canoes for hunters who want to penetrate remote areas often overlooked by others.*

# 12

# Hunting in Bad Weather

It was one of the coldest, wettest mornings I had ever seen in a lifetime of hunting. During the night, a cold front had moved in and the day broke with a steady downpour and bone-chilling temperatures.

I had spent the morning stalk hunting a hardwood-covered ridge where I had been seeing plenty of deer. But on this dreary morning I had failed to see any whitetails, and I was wet and cold. By eleven o'clock I had about all I could take and started down a logging road leading back to my truck.

On the trail, I came upon two other soggy hunters who had also spent a miserable morning without seeing a deer. As we discussed our lack of sanity for hunting under these conditions, I suddenly saw a flicker of movement under some cedars about 75 yards away.

As our conversation continued, I studied the lines under the low-growing trees and suddenly made out three heads. Two does stood with their necks outstretched and their eyes glued to us. Behind them was a buck, his head low to the ground and his antlers laid back. All three were bedded under the thick cedars where little moisture could penetrate. They were convinced we couldn't see them and were holding tight.

I said nothing to the other hunters, and as soon as they walked off, I eased around to a slight ridge to get a shot at the buck. As I edged up to a large oak and started to shoulder my rifle, the does decided I had spotted them and got up running. I never saw where or how the buck left. He just seemed to disappear.

That afternoon, after a hot lunch and a change into dry clothes, I went back into the cold rain. This time I carried a pair of binoculars and started working on a new technique. I looked for any area that would offer deer protection from the constant, cold rain. Whenever I found a low-growing cedar, pine, or other evergreen, I stopped, then spent several minutes scanning every square inch of the cover. I did the same thing for thick cane-breaks, honeysuckle patches, and blowdowns.

I was amazed at the number of deer I found bedded. By three o'clock, one nice buck went home with me as proof that my new bad-weather technique, while requiring a lot of looking and patience, did work.

*Glenn Hegeland was successful despite the foggy, drizzly conditions.*

**Rain**

Since that day several years ago, I have worked to come up with other hunting techniques for those times when rainy weather works against the hunter.

On foggy, drizzly days and during rain storms without much wind, pine plantings draw deer like magnets. The best stands are thick and closely-planted with only two to four feet of ground clearance beneath the lowest branches. Deer will crawl in under the branches and lie down next to the trunk, where the thick boughs provide a nearly waterproof umbrella.

Working as a team, two or three hunters can roust deer from their beds if they are willing to take it slow and quiet. One hunter stalk hunts his way through the pines, weaving from row to row, even belly crawling when necessary. If he is alert and spends time looking at ground level, he'll spot deer parts among the maze of pine branches. When he does, he must decide whether to work into position for a shot or try to push the deer toward his partner(s) who are flanking him on the edge of the planting area. This technique works particularly well in large stands of pine segmented by logging roads, hiking trails, or clearings.

**Snow**

Throughout much of the South, especially where snow is uncommon, an ice or snowstorm can ruin your hunting success. I remember one hunt after a snowstorm had dumped six inches of white stuff on the ground. It was the first snowfall in that area in ten years; there wasn't a deer in those woods that had ever seen snow.

Our camp had 15 hunters and all were anxious for the opportunity to hunt in snow. They were convinced that everyone would get a buck, thanks to the increased visibility and excellent tracking conditions. But by the end of the day, not one deer had been taken. In fact, few shots were fired. The deer were thoroughly spooked and all we saw were a few white tails flashing up ahead. Apparently the deer were frightened by this sudden change in their environment. The cold front following the storm had made the snow noisy to walk in, making it almost impossible to get within sight, much less within shooting distance, of the deer.

The second day we organized a drive covering a large block of land. The technique proved effective, because the spooky deer stayed far out in front of the drivers. The operation produced several bucks, including two of the largest to come out of that area in years.

Another technique that works well during this type of weather, especially on public hunting areas, is to use a tree stand and let the other hunters push deer for you. Go into the woods earlier in the morning than other hunters. Put on some masking scent and take a day pack with enough cold-weather gear to assure a full day on the stand. Penetrate deeper into the woods than most hunters, then set up your tree stand where you can see down into a thick creek bottom or a saddle between two ridges. Let the other hunters do the walking and talking, while you spend the day watching for bucks trying to elude them.

In the North, snow on the ground is welcomed by every hunter who sets foot in the woods. It improves visibility and makes finding "hotspots" much easier. But getting "dumped on" for two or three days in a row can greatly reduce hunting success. Hunters in snow country know that deer movement peaks just

*A light to moderate snowfall can bring ideal hunting conditions. Heavy snows, however, can make hunting tough.*

before and just after a storm. But when a storm is raging, they know that a card game in the cabin may be just as productive as being in the woods. In states with short seasons, however, hunters can ill afford to miss even one hour in the woods.

Drives can be effective if your group is large enough, but if hunting alone, you can still score by relying on the charity of others. One way is to take a stand and allow some other hunter who got *too* cold to push a deer by you. Another is by *pokin'*.

Find a drive that is being conducted and move into a spot on the perimeter of the drive. Ten or 15 minutes after it's started, be in position to walk in behind the drivers. By pokin' along with a crosswind (if the drive was conducted properly it went with the wind), you have a good chance at connecting with a wise old buck who held his ground or slipped back through as the drivers passed.

## Wind

Windy days are often more frustrating than any other type of weather. It may not be as cold, but I usually have a tough time spotting whitetails when the wind is constantly blowing. However, since I advocate hunting every chance you get, I have worked hard to develop a technique that allows me at least a chance of taking a buck on windy days.

Deer are uneasy when the wind is blowing hard—for several reasons. There are a lot of sounds and movements in the woods, plus their keen sense of smell is reduced. They know that their senses of sight, smell, and hearing are not up to par, so they bed down and wait for a lull in the wind before moving around.

On windy days, I prefer to stalk hunt most of the day. I move very slowly into the wind and spend a lot of time looking and waiting. If the wind slackens for a while, I speed up my stalk and try to cover more ground, carefully watching for any movement and listening for any sound.

I try to be especially watchful for bedded deer. In the South, many deer like to bed in openings where broomsedge is growing. They can remain hidden, but can see and hear better than in heavy woods. Many times I have spotted whitetails lying in broomsedge after almost an hour of studying the field with binoculars.

In northern agricultural areas, many deer move into fields of standing corn where the dense stalks shut out the wind. These conditions are perfect for the bowhunter. The rattling corn stalks are noisy, enabling the hunter to move from row to row without being detected. If he spots a whitetail bedded between the corn rows, he can circle around until in position to deliver his arrow.

I like to end a windy day by taking a stand overlooking a field of young oats, wheat, or rye. Often just before dark, a buck will slip out of the woods and into a quiet field to feed for a few brief minutes.

Windy days are also a good time to plan a deer drive. Be sure that your drivers walk with the wind.

It seems that most bad weather comes with an approaching cold front. If the hunter watches the local weather forecast and goes afield before the cold front hits, he will enjoy some easier hunting. Deer know when bad weather is approaching and will feed heavily, even during midday. If you can hunt the day before the cold front, you stand a good chance of getting your deer.

**Safety**

The prime consideration while hunting in bad weather must be safety. Wind shifts and cloudy skies that signal an approaching cold front make getting lost easy, even in familiar country. Especially in areas of mountainous terrain, storms can push in faster than you can get out of the woods. In those situations, personal safety must take priority over hunting. Your hours can be spent more safely and productively studying topo maps and picking the spot where you'll bag a whitetail when the storm lets up.

# 13

# Hunting in Warm Weather

In many states, deer hunting, especially with a bow, opens during warm or even hot weather. This early opening usually brings out concerns for finding whitetails in the heat, along with questions about coping with ticks, mosquitoes, blackflies and poisonous snakes.

One situation that many hunters dislike is a sudden warm spell when the weather should be cold. Unless hunters are willing to change their tactics, they may not see any whitetails during unseasonably hot weather.

Years ago, I remember one warm period that left me totally confused. The deer had virtually disappeared. After that, my hunting partners and I set out to find out why. We started hunting hard during unseasonably hot weather. The lessons we learned came slow and required a lot of time.

Although warm weather offers a nice break after a long cold spell, it appears to cause two changes in deer behavior, especially among bucks. First, I have noticed a dramatic increase in night-feeding. Apparently the cold air in evening makes feeding more pleasant. Second, bucks in low areas seem to hold up in beaver swamps and along creek banks with dense cover. In hilly country, they seem to spend daylight hours in thick, cool cover.

My favorite technique during hot weather is to put a portable stand high in a tree overlooking a creek or swamp. Be in the

*A young hunter heads for home with a nice buck taken during warm weather.*

tree by mid-afternoon and stay alert until dark. Often, deer activity will pick up during the last few minutes of daylight. At this time, a good bright scope can spell the difference between success and failure.

Many of my hunts during warm weather have been along the Tombigbee River in Alabama. I take a stand in thick cover just under the top of the river bank, positioning my stand so I can see down into the tangle. While hunting this area, I have observed deer swimming the wide river. Quite possibly, they enjoy taking to water during hot weather.

Warm weather brings out other problems than just locating deer. Insects can take the enjoyment out of hunting unless you are prepared. Let's look at how to cope with these pests.

## Ticks

Ticks are one of the worst nuisances that hunters encounter during warm weather. There are some 500 different species in the world, with over 100 different types found north of the Mexican border. In fact, there are few dry places where they do not exist.

The three most common types are the Lone Star tick, the American dog tick, and the Rocky Mountain wood tick. Many sportsmen swear there is a fourth type, called the *seed* tick, which is about the size of a pinhead and found in large numbers. In reality, this is the larval stage of one of the above.

Many of the ticks found in the U.S. can transmit germs of several diseases, including Rocky Mountain Spotted Fever (RMSF), a disease that occurs in eastern states as well as in the West.

Everyone should be able to recognize the RMSF symptoms, which appear from 2 to 12 days after being bitten by an infected tick. Early signs are sudden chills, high fever, severe headaches, and other aches and pains. A distinct spotted rash, which may be mistaken for measles, usually appears around the third day of the disease. The rash begins on the wrists, ankles, and back. The illness can be effectively treated with antibiotics, if detected early. Treatment is neither painful nor complicated.

A person may be bitten by a tick without knowing it and later infected with RMSF. At the first sign of these symptoms, call a physician. Make sure he knows the patient was exposed to a tick-infested area. Not all ticks are carriers of RMSF. Even in heavily-infested areas, in fact, only about one tick in 20 is able to transmit the disease.

I can't remember a year when I didn't find a dozen or more ticks on me during the bow season, and I've never suffered any ill effects. But I took a friend on his first hunting trip and he picked up a tick in his hair that he didn't find for several days. Sure enough, he came down with the fever. It didn't discourage him from hunting, but now he keeps a sharp eye out for ticks.

Ticks are found in grass and on bushes, so make it a common practice to check yourself thoroughly at least once each day. Be extra thorough when checking the hairy parts of your body, especially the head.

The first line of defense against ticks is to use a heavy coat of commercial insect repellent which has DEET as its active ingredient. Products with 95 percent DEET seem to work best. Muskol and Ben's 100 contain a high percentage of DEET. If hunting in tick-infested woods, rub the repellent on legs, hands, arms, neck, around the hairline, and around the waist.

It is also a good idea to wear long-sleeved shirts and long pants in tick-infested areas. Keep your pants legs tucked into the boots, or use rubber bands to keep them tight around your boots. Keep shirt sleeves buttoned tight at the wrists, and wear a hat to protect your head.

Following is the recommended way to remove ticks and to treat bites: Coat the tick thoroughly with a petroleum jelly, baby oil, or with a vaporizing salve, such as Vicks VapoRub; or put a drop of gasoline, kerosene, benzine, alcohol, or ether on the general region of the tick's head (or a lighted match or the tip of a burning cigarette) to make it loosen its grip. The tick will take its time releasing its grip, so be patient. It will usually be 10 minutes or so before it drops off. But when it does, it will take its mouthparts with it. A tick also can be killed by covering it with a drop of paraffin or fingernail polish. These substances will seal off the two tiny breathing openings on its sides and suffocate it. *Under no circumstances should an attached tick be squeezed. This will only force more toxin into the bite.*

Once the tick is removed, wash the bite area with soap and water, then apply iodine with some other antiseptic. If a growth or granuloma appears at the site, consult your physician just to be sure that no more serious problems arise. Do this also if signs of infection appear in the bite area.

**Mosquitoes and Blackflies**

In areas where mosquitoes or blackflies are present, use an insect repellent containing at least 95 percent DEET. Of course, the repellent will be a foreign odor to deer, so be even more cautious of wind direction. Also, when using commercial insect repellents, be sure to keep them away from your bow and gun. Chemicals in the repellent will eat away at the finish.

Be sure to apply the repellent to your clothing as well as to your exposed skin. The trick is to apply enough of the repellent to get complete coverage. It takes about five seconds of spray time to cover your arm. Most people try to do it in less than a second.

There are two alternate methods of keeping mosquitoes and blackflies away. When combined with a chemical repellent, these methods can be most effective. The first is to eat one clove of garlic each day. The odor is secreted through the skin and repels insects (as well as your friends).

The second method, one that seems to work well for many people, is taking a dose of vitamin B-1. Those who use this method suggest that you take one, 100 mg vitamin B-1 tablet every six hours while in insect country. Although little research is available on this technique, there are many, including some doctors, who swear it works.

Repellents alone will not give you complete protection from mosquitoes and blackflies in areas of heavy infestations. A head net will be well worth the bother at certain times. One year, while on a caribou hunt in Alaska, I would have gladly traded my custom-made hunting knife for a head net. When the wind wasn't blowing across the tundra, the insects were so thick it was difficult to breathe.

When you are going into bug country, always wear a long-sleeved shirt. Take along some short lengths of cord so you can tie down your shirt sleeves and trouser legs.

Even though you are wearing repellent, some bugs will sneak by your defenses. That's why you should have a lotion such as Campho-Phenique or Calamine Lotion in your first aid kit to apply to the bites. These lotions will minimize the irritation and reduce itching. Another treatment that seems to work for reducing swelling and pain of blackfly bites is placing a pinch of meat tenderizer containing papaya on each bite.

Hunters who camp should learn how to pick a site with insects in mind. Select a campsite away from pools of stagnant water. Pick a site in the open where any breeze will whisk insects away. Always purchase tents that are insect proof and have fine mesh screens. When not going in and out of the tent, keep the screen doors fastened tight. On still, hot nights when mosquitoes are inevitable, plan to set up camp early, before dark, and get to bed early. It's amazing how much you can appreciate a tight, but well ventilated tent.

Occasionally, it may be worth a phone call to check out the insect situation. A few days can make a big difference.

**Poisonous Snakes**

A commonly-asked question among hunters traveling to the Deep South and West for the first time is "How bad are the snakes?" This is probably one of the most overrated fears in the outdoors, yet thousands of hunters don't relax and enjoy their outings simply because of their fear of snakes.

After 20 years of being professionally associated with deer hunting, I know of only five hunters who were bitten by poisonous snakes. We rarely see a snake, much less get bitten. However, there are some basic precautions one should take when hunting in snake country:

Always watch where you are putting your feet, hands, bottom, and face. Look before you reach, step, sit or place your face

*Be careful where you place your feet and hands when in snake country.*

near the ground, a rock outcrop, or bushes. Getting water from a spring is a good way to get bitten in the face, if you don't look first.

Arrive at your campsite early enough in the day, so you have plenty of daylight left to survey the site and to go about setting up camp. Try to pick a site that is free of debris that could harbour snakes. Avoid rock piles and outcroppings, log piles, old houses or buildings, or sites that are weedy or thick with brush. The cleaner the campsite, the better! If you are forced to choose a weedy campsite, take the time to trim the weeds around the area. Keep alert while doing so. Remember, snakes like cover; a campsite that is clean will discourage the critters.

Keep as much of your gear as possible off the ground and stored neatly. Keep your tent closed tightly during the day, especially if it has screen doors. Hang sleeping bags up well off the ground to air. Sloppy campers give snakes plenty of cover and invite them to come in.

If you must move around your campsite at night, do so only with a good light. Examine every step before you take it. Remember that most snakes prefer to travel at night, a good time for you to sit around the fire or catch up on some sleep.

It is a common practice among campers to turn over their canoes or boats at the end of the day. But an overturned craft near water makes a good resting site for a cottonmouth. Be cautious as you turn the boat upright and make sure you don't have a stowaway coiled under the bow, stern, or seat. You don't want to discover an unwanted passenger after you shove off.

Proper treatment of a poisonous snakebite has long been one of the most disputed subjects in the medical profession. I discussed the subject with doctors knowledgeable in the field of snakebites. Two of the best known are Dr. Charles Watt of Thomasville, Georgia, with whom I worked when writing my book on *Swamp Camping*, and Dr. Robert Sheppard of Carrollton, Alabama, an expert in survival medicine and an experienced outdoorsman. These doctors advocate the following treatment:

1) Get away from the snake. It is not unusual for a snake to bite the victim several times.

2) Try to remain calm.

3) Positively identify the snake, and if possible, get someone to kill it so you can take it to the doctor for positive identification. That knowledge will be helpful in the treatment.

4) Make a constricting band out of a handkerchief, shoestring, shirt sleeve, sock, or belt. Put this band above the bite (that is, between the bite and the body). It should be so loose that you can easily insert a finger under it. Such a constricting band will not stop the flow of blood through the artery, but it does check the return of blood through the veins, which slows the spread of venom. Do not loosen this constricting band.

5) If you are within an hour's travel to a doctor, prepare the victim for the trip. Immobilize the bitten limb by putting on a splint. Make sure, however, that the splint's bindings are loose so they do not impair circulation. If possible, keep the limb horizontal. The victim should not walk unless absolutely necessary; other members of the group should carry the victim to the vehicle or boat.

6) If more than an hour away from a doctor, follow this procedure, provided it can be done within the first five minutes after the bite: Wash the wound with water, soap, alcohol, or whatever you have on hand. Make a short, approximately ½-inch, straight incision (no cross cut) over each fang mark. Cut vertically with the limb. The cut should be no deeper than the fatty tissue under the skin. That is usually one-quarter of an inch.

Use an instrument that has been sterilized in the flame of a match and is razor sharp.

7)   If you have no cuts or sores in your mouth, suck the wound vigorously, or have someone else do it, if he can do so safely. Suction can remove 20 to 50 percent of the venom. A suction cup from a snakebite kit is useful if you are alone and the bite is in an area you cannot reach with your mouth. It is important that you do not delay the trip to the doctor in order to cut and suck. Do this en route. To delay the injection of antivenin is to risk death.

8)   Apply a constricting band and a splint as directed earlier, and get medical treatment as quickly as possible.

Other points to remember concerning snakebite:

Never give a snakebite victim alcohol. It speeds up the flow of blood through the system and hastens the effect of the bite.

Immediately remove rings, bracelets, watches, shoes, or whatever from a bitten limb. The swelling will be fast, and such objects will constrict.

Absence of pain, swelling, or other symptoms does not necessarily mean that no venom has been injected. Bites that at first seem superficial can be fatal.

Most hospitals in snake country have antivenin for the treatment of snakebite. If a hospital doesn't have antivenin, they can call the Arizona Poison Center at (602) 626-6016 24 hours a day. They maintain a computerized inventory of antivenin available across the nation. I keep this phone number taped in the lid of my first-aid kit. Most likely I'll never need it, but it's there if I should.

The odds are great that you will spend a lifetime hunting and never see a person bitten by a poisonous snake. However, the potential does exist and caution should be taken. By following these rules and using a little common sense, you should never be bothered.

# 14

# Ten Tips to Increase Your Success

S everal years ago, I began studying deer hunters who are successful year in and year out. It soon became apparent that certain hunters weren't just lucky. They took their hunting seriously and worked hard to get it down to a science. In talking with these hunters, I learned that all pay a great deal of attention to the fine points of deer hunting. And, almost to the man, they take extra steps to swing the odds in their favor. These details are often overlooked by the novice or casual hunter.

Here are 10 of these fine points for deer hunting that might help you bag a wall-hanger.

1) *Determine wind direction.* Most hunters know that a knowledge of wind direction is beneficial to their success and that it is necessary to hunt downwind from deer. However, many overlook the fact that even when it appears calm, there generally is a slight breeze. One way to determine wind direction on an apparently quiet day is to tie a four-inch length of sewing thread to the top of your bow or the front swivel of your rifle. The thread will indicate the direction of even the lightest breeze.

2) *Paint your tree stand.* Not long ago, a hunter asked me to check out his tree stand to see if I could tell what he was doing wrong. After three days of hunting, he had not seen a deer. I asked him to climb up to his stand so I could figure out what was awry. Once he was in his stand, I suddenly noticed the problem—

*This muzzleloader hunter has painted the bottom of his stand a dark color.*

the shiny white bottom of the stand. He had done an excellent job of painting the top side so it blended with the surroundings, but it never occurred to him to paint the snow-white bottom. This may not have been the only reason he was skunked, but it was an important area he had overlooked. Smart hunters camouflage the underside of their platforms.

3) *Wear yellow shooting glasses.* Many experts who kill large deer consistently wear yellow shooting glasses when they hunt in dense timber. When hunting during periods of low light, the glasses enable you to see much more clearly. They are also helpful for scouting whitetails, allowing you to better detect sign as well as deer movements. And finally, they protect your eyes from thorns and sharp branches.

4) *Use binoculars.* Any hunter who takes his deer hunting seriously will invest in a pair of quality binoculars and use them regularly. I have spotted many deer with my binoculars, particularly during periods of low light, such as early in the morning or toward sunset. Binoculars are especially handy when hunting around large agricultural fields.

5) *Keep your muscles loose.* Sitting still in a tree stand or in a ground blind can tighten up your muscles. I make it a practice, whether in a blind or stand, to take a few moments each hour to stretch slowly, move my arms and legs, draw my bow, or point my rifle to flex my muscles. The hunter who sits like a statue in a cold stand will find it difficult to quickly draw his bow or shoot his rifle when the time comes.

6) *Rain-proof your rifle.* Rainy weather has a tendency to send many hunters, especially those with expensive firearms, back to their vehicles. A trick I learned from hunting guide Earl Gates comes in handy for protecting your rifle during a rain. When a storm threatens, Earl simply goes back to his truck, pulls the dipstick out of the engine block, then wipes oil from the dipstick onto his rifle. The thin coating of oil protects the rifle, regardless of how hard it rains.

7) *Wear a headnet and gloves.* My years of turkey hunting have helped me to become a better deer hunter. For example, I have learned that by wearing a camouflage headnet and cotton camouflage gloves, I see many more deer than I did in the past. The headnet not only camouflages my skin, it traps warm air, keeping my face and head much warmer. The mesh is fine enough, however, so I can still see what's going on in the woods.

8) *Make your practice shots count.* Shortly after they arrive at my hunting lodges, many hunters head for the rifle range where they shoot at a bull's eye-type target three or four times, then declare themselves ready to hunt. But when they get the opportunity to shoot a whitetail, they miss.

Hunters who want to be successful should spend time on the rifle or archery range weeks before the season begins. Also, shoot the exact cartridge and load on the practice range that you will use when hunting.

9) *Watch for squirrels.* In early fall, when scouting for mast-producing trees that attract deer, pay attention to squirrel movements and feeding areas. Squirrels, like deer, prefer those trees on which acorns are plentiful. If you find oak trees that contain squirrels, then you have probably found an area where deer also feed.

10) *Check for trail use.* One of the best ways to see if a trail is being used is an old trick of many expert deer hunters. On their scouting trips, they take along a spool of dark sewing thread. At

*Good deer hunters practice their shooting skills, whether they use a firearm or bow and arrow.*

several locations, they tie strands of thread about three feet above the trail, then check the strands periodically. If a thread is broken, the direction in which the two ends are lying will usually reveal which way the deer was walking. The more you can set and check threads, the more you know about the extent of deer movements.

These fine points of deer hunting, along with the major points that we have discussed throughout the book, can often make the difference between success and failure. Take them seriously and you'll take home more venison.

# 15

# Making One Shot Count

E ach year millions of hunters spend millions of dollars on hunting equipment. They devote countless hours to packing and adjusting their gear. Then, the big day arrives. The first morning out, a large buck comes into view—the moment of truth is at hand. A shot is fired and the buck disappears, unharmed, back into the bush. A whole year of preparation and anticipation was hanging on that one shot, but the hunter failed to make it count. Had the hunter devoted some time prior to the season learning to make the one-shot kill, this story would have had a happy ending.

Our forefathers knew how to make one-shot kills, because the limitations of the muzzleloading rifle demanded it. Modern-day bowhunters and muzzleloaders have revived this skill and now serious rifle, shotgun, and handgun hunters are practicing so they can make that first, all-important shot.

## Sighting In

Sight in your bow or firearm during the latter part of summer. Be sure you have the right equipment to shoot accurately. If there is any doubt, don't hesitate to seek assistance from an archery or shooting club. Many sporting goods stores will help check out your equipment.

*One-shot kills begin with
practice sessions at the
shooting range.*

Once you have the right equipment, begin shooting at a range. Know your firearm's or bow's capability. Shoot regularly and learn where to hold on the target at all distances within a reasonable range. Do not accept mediocrity when sighting in your gun or bow. Keep working until you know it will shoot where you aim it.

To some degree, most hunters carry out this first step. However, very few train themselves any further. Confident they can hit a bull's eye from a benchrest, they stop practicing and wait for the deer season. Not the serious hunter. He continues shooting and moves on to the second phase of his training.

### Practice Shooting

Step number two will take some time and practice. I know of no hunters who take deer from a benchrest or indoor archery range. Once you have your bow or gun sighted in and you are hitting consistently, start shooting from the various positions you may encounter during your hunt.

The tree stand has become one of our most important hunting tools, but have you ever practiced shooting from one? Place your stand on the edge of your range and begin shooting from different positions. Suddenly, you will see why you may have missed shots in the past. It takes a lot of time and practice to shoot consistently well with your body twisted at different angles. Not only are you improving your ability to hold steady and fire accurately, you are also gaining confidence and learning to shoot safely.

If you like to take a ground stand and watch deer trails or feeding areas, practice shooting from a sitting or standing position. Holding steady can be difficult from these positions and much practice is needed to become accurate.

If you are a stalk hunter, practice from the standing and kneeling positions. Learn how to use a post or tree to support your rifle, making your aim much steadier.

### Judging Distance

It never ceases to amaze me how so many hunters misjudge the distance of deer. This alone accounts for a high percentage of missed shots. If you cannot tell whether a buck is 50 or 150 yards away, you won't bring home many trophies, if any.

One of the best ways to learn how to judge distance is to practice shooting at life-size deer silhouettes or paper deer targets at an unknown distance. Find a woods or range where you have a safe impact area, then have a friend set up six life-size deer targets, the type bowhunters practice on, at varying distances. Ask him to number each target. The ranges should be from 50 to 200 yards if you shoot a rifle, 10 to 40 yards for a bow. Spread out the targets so that some are at an angle. Have your friend stand behind you and call a number. You have five seconds to find the right deer, estimate the distance, and get off your shot at a vital area. It won't take long to get the hang of judging distance, especially if your friend is trying to outshoot you.

*Hunters can improve their ability to judge distance by practice-shooting at life-size deer targets.*

*This hunter has put a shot into the lung area just behind the heart. The dotted area above his hand denotes the liver.*

To keep yourself in tune, try to judge distances everyday. While walking down the street, pick out a telephone pole, parking meter, or parked car, guess the distance, then count your paces. Did you come close? This type of practice will pay off many times during your hunts.

Modern technology has also stepped in to help the hunter determine distances. Ranging, Inc., a company which manufactures measuring systems, has developed a series of compact rangefinders that will help you identify the distance to your trophy. Also, most scope manufacturers have models with built-in rangefinders.

### Know the Vital Areas of Deer
Hunters must learn the vital areas of deer so they know exactly where to aim, thus insuring a one-shot kill.

It is the responsibility of each hunter to make a clean kill. The hunter who sees a big buck, throws up his rifle, and shoots at the deer in general is a poor excuse for a hunter. No hunter should ever pull the trigger of his rifle or release his bow string unless he is aiming for a deer's vitals.

Your first step in learning the location of the vital area is to study a picture or target on which the region is outlined. Most hunters think the vital area is higher and larger than it actually is. Memorize the lung area and how the shoulder covers part of the lung. A bullet smashing the shoulder and driving pieces of bone into the lungs will stop a deer fast. Note the locations of arteries, spine, and liver. Note the size of the vital area when deer stand at different angles to you, such as broadside or quartering away.

Next, go to a zoo or private game farm and study live deer. Visualize where you would aim. Check yourself with a vital areas chart.

Your final step should be to order several life-size deer targets with the vital area outlined. You can order the targets from any of several bowhunting supply houses. Set up the targets on your gun or bow range at the distance you sighted in. Draw a bead on the vital area and shoot at it. Check the target to see if you are placing your shots in the correct spot. Practice until you

*When the "moment of truth" finally comes, put your practice to work and make your first shot count. Remaining calm is important to a steady aim.*

are confident that you can hit the vital area with your first shot. And, be sure to take some practice shots from your tree stand and from sitting, standing and kneeling positions.

## Making the Shot

The last step in mastering the one-shot kill is to practice over and over again what you will do with a trophy buck in your sights. Learn to go through a mental checklist. Is it a legal buck? How far away is it? Are you in a good shooting position? Can you hit a vital area from this angle? With these questions answered, take a deep breath, try to remain calm, and put good marksmanship to work.

All this sounds simple and easy, but many experienced hunters cannot put it all together when the time comes. They shoot at deer too far away, they fail to aim for a vital area, or they are unable to hold steady.

The art of making a one-shot kill requires a lot of practice and self-discipline. But the final reward is worth the effort. To make a clean, quick kill is the mark of a true sportsman.

# 16

# After the Shot

I grew up under the hunting tutorship of a father who believed in making every shot count and finding wounded game no matter how long it took. We spent many hours searching for fallen squirrels, while other animals played in the not-too-distant trees. We found our game before continuing the hunt.

This was good training and it carried through to my deer hunting. As a professional guide, I see many hunters who are unable to recognize a hit and do not know how to follow up a wounded deer. When I see this, somewhere in my mind I hear my dad saying, "Stay with the game until you find it."

Regardless of how well you shoot, if you do much deer hunting you are going to have to track down a fair percentage of the deer you hit. A buck hit in the heart or lungs may travel several hundred yards before it drops. Once you hit a deer, your duties as a responsible hunter are clear-cut. You must make every effort to recover the animal.

Once you find a big buck, aim and shoot, the work is not over—it is just beginning. When the gun goes off or you release your arrow, be alert and watch the animal. Did he drop? If not, did you hear a thump when the bullet or slug or broadhead hit? Did he throw up his tail and disappear in a flash? If he did, you probably have a clean miss. Did he hunch and lope off with his tail down? If so, your bullet probably hit the gut area. Did he run off staggering, looking weak and with his tail down? This usually indicates a good, solid hit.

The tail is a good clue to watch. In most cases, a whitetail that has been hit, but not knocked down, will run off with its tail down.

Regardless of whether or not you dropped the buck, the first thing to do is reload your firearm or nock another arrow. An arrow may pass through a non-vital area of a deer, such as the stomach region, and the animal will show little reaction. You may need another quick arrow to finish the job. Many firearms hunters have dropped a big buck, and in their excitement, run up to the animal without reloading. When they got to the buck, it suddenly lurched to its feet and ran off, leaving them watching helplessly.

The best way to approach a downed whitetail is from his back, so if he is alive, he won't see you. Then, with gun or bow in a ready position, cautiously move around until you can see his eyes. The eyes will reveal if there is any life left in him. If they have a glazed, dull look, the deer is dead. If bright and shiny, he is still alive and another shot will usually be necessary. A supposedly-dead whitetail can be dangerous if he suddenly comes alive as you prepare to field-dress him.

If the buck ran off after your shot, remain calm. As we said, reload and recall the animal's reaction. Before leaving your shooting spot, mentally mark where the deer was standing when you hit him. Seasoned bowhunters shoot an arrow into the area. Pick out several landmarks, so you can walk directly to the spot. Also, mark where you were standing, because you may need to re-enact the shot to determine where to pick up the deer's trail. Many hunters carry a roll of toilet tissue in their hunting coat, for obvious reasons, but also for marking a trail while tracking a wounded deer.

Once you have marked your shooting spot, walk to where the deer was standing. Look for the tracks he made when running off. Use a compass to get a bearing on his direction. Also, look for signs of a hit such as hair, blood, fat, bone splinters, etc. If you find any of these signs, mark the area with several sheets of toilet tissue. This will be your starting point for tracking the animal.

Now you will want to wait for 30 minutes to allow the deer to get sick, bed down, and weaken from bleeding. If you start after him immediately, you will scare him into running and make

*If you down a whitetail, quickly reload, then approach the animal from the rear.
Then, move to where you can check the deer's eyes for any sign of life.*

your tracking job much tougher. There are, however, two exceptions to this rule. First, if it is raining, you have no choice but to follow before the blood trail washes away. Second, if there are many other hunters in the area, you may want to pursue the animal in the hopes of finding it before another hunter stumbles across it.

While waiting, think of your situation as a mystery—to solve it, you will need every clue you can get. Begin by examining any hair you find. A deer's hair can provide clues to where you hit the animal, because each part of the hide has its own distinct hairs. Here are typical samples you may find:

*Heart.* Long, dark guard hairs found only in this area. It may be graying on older deer.

*Spine.* Long, coarse, hollow hairs that are dark with black tips.

*Brisket.* Curly, coarse hair that is stiff and somewhat black.

*Tail.* Long, coarse, and wavy hair that is dark to light brown on top and white underneath.

*Stomach.* Coarse, hollow hair that is brownish gray with light tips.

This is only a sample for your consideration. The best way to

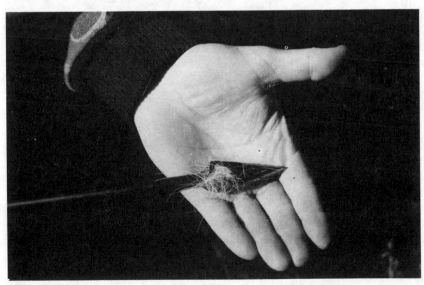

**The type of hair can reveal where your arrow or bullet struck the deer.**

learn to distinguish the different hair characteristics is to study a deer rug.

Blood can also tell you a lot about the hit. Blood from the heart, arteries, or liver will appear dark maroon. A flesh wound is light red, about the color you expect blood to be. Lung blood is easy to identify because it contains pink foam or tiny bubbles. A gut shot will leave a light-colored blood, usually with greenish bile or digestive material mixed in.

By combining the way the deer reacted with bits of hair and spots of blood, most experienced hunters can determine where they hit the deer and if they stand a good chance of finding it.

Generally, here is what you can expect from the various hits:

*Stomach or gut.* Under good tracking conditions, an experienced hunter who is positive that he made a gut shot will wait six to eight hours before starting to track the animal. He may stay on the trail for up to two days.

*Heart.* You will find that the amount of blood increases as you follow the trail. Usually, you will find the animal dead within 100 yards.

*Spine.* When hit in the spine, a deer drops in its tracks.

*Lung.* There may be no blood at first, but after the lung fills up, the deer will begin to leave a good blood trail. The animal will probably travel up to 400 yards.

*Back.* Back shots in the loin, kidney, or aortic artery are usually fatal. You will probably find the deer within 100 yards.

*Neck.* If the neck shot does not hit the spine, windpipe, or jugular, the deer may recover. However, if hit in any one of these vital areas, he will not move farther than 50 yards.

*Brisket.* Unless he was facing you when shot, he will live. If he was moving toward you, the bullet or arrow passed through the brisket and probably hit the lung or heart. The blood will tell you what to expect.

*Hindquarter.* Unless the bullet or arrow hit the femoral artery (located just under the skin on the inside of the leg), you are in for a long tracking session and you may have to shoot the animal again. If you hit the artery, you will usually find him within one-half mile.

## How to Trail a Wounded Deer

While waiting to trail a wounded deer, you may want to enlist the help of a hunting buddy. As you trail the animal, one can study the ground for blood and tracks, while the other constantly scans the area ahead. If following a deer that is only lightly wounded, it is important that you spot him before he detects you. A surprisingly large number of hunters are red color-blind. If you are among them, you definitely will need another set of eyes to follow the blood trail. On the other hand, don't get more than two hunters involved—a crowd may destroy valuable signs.

As you follow the trail, leave a piece of toilet tissue at each blood spot. The string of tissues will serve as a reference for helping you line up the deer's direction. Also, the last piece of tissue may become your starting point if you lose the trail. If that happens, look back at the pieces of paper. The line of paper should point you in the general direction the deer is heading, enabling you to pinpoint your search efforts.

Be careful when looking for the blood trail. You may be destroying it as you walk or covering it up by kicking leaves over the spots. Watch for blood on low-hanging tree branches, shrubs, or tall weeds. A lung shot or high body shot will sometimes spray blood up to three feet above the ground. If you are having trouble finding blood, or if the deer is moving in a zig-zag pattern, search for sign in a 20-yard circle. Examine every leaf, blade of grass,

*Marking a blood trail with toilet paper makes finding a hit deer much easier.*

***Author Fears uses a gas lantern to blood-trail a whitetail.***

and rock; you should be able to pick up the trail again.

Blood scattered over leaves, rocks, and the soil indicates the direction the buck is moving. As he runs, the blood splatters in the direction he is traveling. When he is standing, the blood falls straight down and makes a circle.

For many years, hunters believed that wounded deer always travel downhill. Don't believe it. They go uphill as much, if not more, than downhill. More times than not, a wounded deer will make for water if there is any nearby. No one is certain as to why they head for water; possibly because they feel thirsty. Also, it is not unusual for a wounded animal to lie down, then use his front hooves to stuff leaves and grass into the wound.

A whitetail will generally make his getaway by following the path of least resistance. It may be a deer trail, old logging road, or a thin strip of woods. If unaware that he is being followed, he will slow down to a walk. When he begins to weaken, he will usually find a thick clump of bushes in which to lie down.

For some unknown reason, many deer circle back to the same general area where they were shot. Hunters have trailed deer through the night, only to find them dead the next morning a few yards from where they were shot.

If your tracking goes on into the night, be sure to carry a gas lantern. Many hunters and guides prefer to track wounded deer at night with a gas lantern, because the light makes the blood spots stand out, almost to the point of glowing. A hunter who does a lot of late-afternoon hunting should always carry a gas lantern in his vehicle. Before you trail a deer at night, check your state hunting regulations. In many states, it is illegal to carry a bow or firearm into the woods at night.

All hunters should learn how to blood-trail a deer. Many bowhunters practice the technique before the season begins. They make artificial blood by combining eight ounces of glycerine with two ounces of water and 3/4-ounce of red food coloring. They pour the blood-like liquid into a plastic detergent container so it can be squirted out like blood dropping from a wounded deer. Have your hunting partner lay out a blood trail and practice following it. Many hunting clubs are conducting blood-trailing sessions as part of their pre-season activities.

It takes as much, if not more skill and woods knowledge to successfully track a wounded deer than it does to find a whitetail in the first place. A hunter is measured by his ability to stick to the trail of a wounded animal until it is found.

# 17

# Success Comes with the Right Equipment

W hen I first started deer hunting in the 1950s, I was in college and had no money to spend on equipment. Little did I know that my worn-out Army surplus gear was reducing my hunting success. When it rained, I got wet; when it was cold, I was too cold to concentrate on hunting. Most of my equipment was noisy. My knife was better suited for defending the Alamo than for dressing out a deer.

Today, there is little excuse for the deer hunter to have inadequate or broken-down equipment. Modern technology offers us products that are quiet, warm, safe, waterproof, highly effective, and best of all, available within a moderate price range. Following are my thoughts and recommendations based on years of trial-and-error experience:

## Hunting Rifles

The best type and caliber of rifle for hunting deer has been debated among hunters and shooting experts for decades. Entire books are devoted to the subject, but for the sake of brevity, here is what I have come to trust after 20 years of hunting and seeing scores of other hunters shoot deer.

My first observation is that there is no such thing as a rifle that will accurately shoot a bullet through brush. The so-called brush-bucking rifle does not exist. All bullets will deflect off branches and twigs, and contrary to what many hunters believe, slower-moving bullets deflect more than high-velocity bullets.

My second observation is that 7mm magnums and .300 magnums with hot factory loads are too powerful for whitetails. I once had to blood-trail six wounded bucks over the course of one evening. All were shot late in the afternoon with the big magnums. As we found them one by one, we discovered that the over powered bullets passed through the animals without leaving much energy. The bucks covered a lot of ground before they died.

For my own hunting, I have come to trust the .243 Win. shooting a 100-grain bullet for small to average deer (150-pound average). If I'm after a big buck over 150 pounds, I use a .30-06 with a 150-grain bullet. This combination has worked well for years. Other good calibers for whitetails include: .30-30 Win., .270 Win., .280 Rem., 7 × 57 Mauser, and .308 Win.

As for the type of rifle action, my suggestion is to use the one which you can fire most accurately. I prefer a bolt-action rifle, such as the Remington 700 or Winchester 70. Single-shot and bolt actions have the most rigid construction and have fewer moving parts than other actions, which theoretically makes them

*Author Fears with a hefty whitetail buck taken with a Mauser-action, .30-06 In-terarms rifle with a Simmons 3 × 9 variable power scope.*

the most accurate. But usually it isn't the action that determines accuracy—it's you. Confidence is the key, so use a rifle that you know you can shoot well.

## Rifle Scopes

I know for a fact that you will take more deer if you have a scope on your rifle. Modern scopes enable you to hunt from several minutes to more than one hour longer each day because of their light-gathering properties. Several hunters at my lodges have taken bucks sneaking into wheat fields just before dark. They were using my rifles with Simmons 3-9X scopes. Each hunter told me that without the scope, he would never have seen the buck.

## Bows and Arrows

Hunting whitetails with bow and arrow is currently undergoing a surge in popularity. One reason for this growth is that today's bowhunter is outfitted with the finest equipment in the history of archery.

There are many types of bows and arrows available to the hunter. Before you make a selection, seek the advice of someone experienced in the sport and ask for his personal recommendations. The bowhunter with mismatched equipment has two strikes against him before he goes into the woods. Most cities have first-class archery shops with top professionals who are willing to help you. Many of these shops have practice ranges, where you can try out different types of archery equipment. You can also get assistance at an archery or bowhunting club.

Hunting bows fall into three general categories: recurves, compounds, and long bows. The recurve bow, which has lost much of its popularity since the invention of the compound, should be at least 45 pounds in pull. The compound bow, which for many hunters is much easier to use, should have at least 40 pounds pull, although many hunters favor a 55- to 65-pound range. More and more hunters are taking up the long bow, which is similar to those we see in old Robin Hood movies. Most long bows are quite hard to pull and hold, and require a great deal of practice.

The arrows you select should be matched with the bow—in other words, the more powerful the bow, the stiffer the arrow. No matter which type of broadhead you use, make sure the blades are sharp enough to shave the hair on your arm. An arrow kills

*Fears used a Bear compound bow to take this buck near a scrape.*

primarily by hemorrhage; a dull broadhead tends to push vital organs aside rather than cutting them cleanly.

Other archery equipment you will need includes camouflage clothing; a quiver, which either fits on the bow or on the hunter's belt to hold the arrows; a shooting glove; and an armguard.

### Shotguns

In the Deep South, many areas are so thickly vegetated that hunters use dogs and shotguns with buckshot to take whitetails. In a number of northern states and particularly in heavily-populated counties, laws require hunters to use shotguns and slugs.

The serious whitetail hunter should not consider anything but a 12 or 10 gauge gun in order to assure himself of a clean kill. Most hunters prefer a short, 18 to 26-inch barrel with an improved cylinder or cylinder bore, and adjustable rifle sights installed at the factory. Joe LaBarbera, father of *North American Hunter* Senior Vice President Mark LaBarbera, uses a 3-9X scope on his Remington 1100 to see deer in brush and low light during the Wisconsin season. The hunter using a shotgun and slugs can expect to be fairly accurate out to 100 yards.

Popular shotguns for shooting slugs include the Browning Auto-5 Buck Special which has a 24-inch barrel; the Ithaca Mag-10 Deerslayer with a 22-inch barrel; and the Remington 1100 deer gun with a 22-inch barrel.

Hunters who use buckshot where it is legal prefer a full choke shotgun. Most prefer #1 buckshot, with 00 buck and 0 buck ranking as second and third choices. Your effective range is only about 40 yards; shots beyond this distance should be avoided. Before you shoot buckshot for deer, spend some time at the pattern board learning the range of your shotgun and its shot pattern. Many hunters do not take careful aim at their target; consequently, many deer are wounded by buckshot each year.

## Hunting Knives

I probably get more mail from hunters concerning knives than any other subject. Far too many think it takes a 10-inch combat knife to field-dress a deer. The truth is that a quality-made hunting knife with a four-inch blade will do the job nicely. When field-dressing or skinning a deer, rarely will you use more than the two inches of blade near the tip.

One of the most popular blade shapes is the "drop-point", which makes it relatively easy to field-dress an animal without splitting the stomach. The drop-point blade also works well for skinning. Other common blade shapes include the clip type and the upward-curved skinning blade. Because only a small portion of the blade is used, many whitetail hunters are switching from fixed-type knives with long blades to folding knives with shorter blades.

## Binoculars

A good pair of binoculars is a must item for all hunters. If you do not use them, you are probably overlooking many whitetails. The current trend in selecting binoculars is to think small. Many hunters like compact types that are easy to carry, but don't sacrifice magnification. High-quality binoculars such as Bushnell, Simmons, or Steiner offer several good models. I have come to trust a Simmons armored 8 x 24 compact binoculars. The armored coating does not make a metallic sound when bumped against a rifle or tree stand, and the dull color aids in my total camouflage.

*Spotting scopes, such as this model by Simmons, are ideal for locating whitetails at long distances. Be sure to select a steady rest or the image will be blurred.*

## Spotting Scopes

We commonly think of the spotting scope as an essential item for hunting pronghorns, elk, and sheep. However, many deer hunters who work expanses of open or semi-open lands or mountainous terrain use spotting scopes. In the Midwest, for example, hunters locate and observe deer crossing fields of corn or alfalfa. Western hunters spot trophy bucks bedding along canyon edges and river valleys.

Spotting scopes such as those made by Simmons, Bushnell, Redfield, and other optic companies enable hunters to examine trophies at a distance, where they will not spook the animals. Pinpointing the locations of a distant whitetail gives you ample time to study the terrain and plan a stalk that will bring you within good shooting range of the animal.

## Compass

The well-equipped deer hunter should always carry a compass and know how to use it. A compass not only keeps you from becoming lost, but it can be a useful tool for trailing a wounded deer or marking good hunting areas on a topographic map for future trips.

Several excellent compasses are available; however, a model made by Silva appears to be made especially for the deer hunter. The Silva Landmark Type 27 is a small, 1½ x 2-inch compact compass. It has a sighting mirror, sun watch, protractor base plate with a one-inch map scale, and luminous points for night-time use.

One of the most convenient compasses I have used is a skin-diver's compass made by the Dacor Corporation. This high-quality compass slips easily onto a watchband and is always handy for instant reading. It is so convenient that I have permanently attached one to my watchband.

## Hunting Clothes

Now, let's take an inside-out look at the hunter's clothing, including some of the latest products on the market.

*Underwear.* Several styles and types are available to keep you warm in cold, damp weather. My favorite is made from 100 percent polypropylene, a fabric that has very little bulk, allows moisture to escape, and has the lowest thermal conductivity of all natural and man-made fibers. My second choice is the two-layered, cotton-wool underwear made by Duofold. Both brands

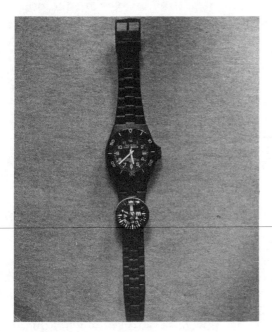

*This model of compass can be permanently attached to your watchband.*

are available from mail-order houses such as Eddie Bauer or Early Winters.

*Sweaters.* One of the warmest and quietest hunting garments is the all-wool sweater known as the Woolley Pully. It is made by Brigade Quartermasters, Ltd. Wearing this sweater over a shirt may be all you need on a cold day, provided the wind isn't blowing. As a rule, wool sweaters are not good wind-breakers. But what they lack as a wind-breaker, they more than make up for in quietness when stalk hunting through brush, and warmth, even when wet. I am especially fond of a forest green Woolley Pully for stalk hunting.

Another selection of high-quality sweaters is made by Winona Camo. These sweaters are available in a brown camouflage and a hunter orange/black camouflage pattern that meets the requirements of most hunting regulations. The company also makes knit vests, hats, and trousers which offer the hunter warmth and quietness along with concealment.

*Coats.* Among the greatest advancements in hunting wear is in the area of coats. Companies such as Himalayan, Red Head, Browning, Game Winner, and many others offer a wide variety of coats designed with the deer hunter in mind.

We are now seeing companies getting away from the noisy nylon shell and going to an outer layer made from quieter material, such as wool, or a blend of cotton/nylon or cotton poplin.

For warmth, there is a wide variety of insulating fibers available. Down, Hollofil, Thermal R, Quallofil, and Thinsulate are just a few of the insulators used in hunting coats. The hunter would be well-advised to study the qualities and weak points of each insulator. For example, how well does it hold up when wet? Down loses most of its insulating quality when wet, which can become a serious problem when hunting far from your camp or car. When purchasing a coat, buy from a reputable sporting goods dealer who knows the conditions in which you hunt and can match your needs to a certain type of insulation.

Color of the hunting coat is important. Hunter orange is required for firearms hunters in most states and provinces. Early-season bowhunters want green camouflage. I have also been using the Trebark camouflage and find it to work exceptionally well for both gun and bow seasons. Most sporting goods dealers can offer high-quality coats in any of these patterns.

The secret to making a wise purchase is to know what qualities you want before you shop. Next, stay with well-known brand names and buy the best coat you can afford. A cheap coat that doesn't allow you to hunt comfortably can cost you several big bucks, and I'm speaking of the deer type.

*Trousers.* Deer hunting trousers vary almost as much as do deer hunters. I still see a large number of hunters wearing blue jeans, which is okay if you stay dry and they aren't so tight that you can't sit down. There are some excellent trousers available to the deer hunter, both insulated and non-insulated, in hunter orange, and brown, green, or Trebark camouflage. For instance, Red Head makes hunting trousers of heavy-duty, water-repellent cotton with a rubberized overlay. These trousers are full-cut for active wear, like using a climbing tree stand. Game Winner has a nylon-faced camouflage pants which features a waterproof seat.

Many deer hunters in the snow-belt states still prefer to wear full-cut, wool trousers. I have to agree with their reasons. Trousers such as those sold by L.L. Bean and Eddie Bauer are quiet, durable, warm even when wet, and when loosely worn, do not cut off circulation.

*Gloves.* For a very small investment, usually under $10, you can keep your hands warm on the coldest of mornings. Wells Lamont, a well-known glove manufacturer, makes gloves in hunter orange, brown, and green camouflage. A glove especially suited for the deer hunter is the Sharpshooter. It is 100 percent wool with a deerskin leather index and middle finger for shooting. It also has a full-webbed, knit wrist for added warmth.

*Headwear.* Caps and hats are the in-thing these days— hundreds of companies are using camouflage caps as a form of advertising. During warm weather, a camouflage or hunter orange cap with a mesh top is sufficient. But for cold weather, I prefer a hunter orange wool stocking cap, sometimes called a watch cap. Whatever type you choose, make sure it can be pulled down over your ears. Remember, you can lose as much as 50 percent of your body heat through an uncovered head—a loss you can ill-afford.

*Boots.* Hunters can select from many excellent models of hunting boots. The choice of boot is as individual as the choice of gun. I have come to depend upon two pairs for my deer hunting.

In warm weather and for stalk hunting, I wear a well-broken-in pair of Browning featherweight boots. These high-quality

*Author is dressed for a late-season muzzleloader hunt. Note his wool Balaclava-type cap, which can be pulled down over the face and neck.*

boots allow me to move quietly in the woods. In cold weather, I like the Timberland waterproof insulated boots. Although they are relatively expensive, I have spent days hunting in snow without getting cold or wet feet.

How well you take care of your boots may be just as important as the type you choose. Keep your boots water repellent with a wax-type compound like Sno-Seal. Greases and oils soak into the leather and reduce its natural insulating properties. Many seasoned hunters buy their cold-weather boots one size larger than normal, so they can comfortably wear two pairs of wool socks.

The equipment you select for deer hunting will have a great deal of bearing on your success. Take your time, shop around, and buy high-quality equipment that is ideal for the conditions in which you hunt. Learn how to use your equipment properly and take care of it. In the long run, it will be a good investment.

# 18

# Scents and Lures

Whitetail deer and their habits are undergoing a current up-surge of research by many sportsmen, game and fish agencies, and universities. One area that is being researched with an interest toward improving the luck of hunters is measuring the effectiveness of various kinds of scents.

It is well documented that the whitetail's best line of defense is its keen sense of smell. Many hunters go into the woods year after year without seeing a deer, and especially a buck. It wasn't because deer numbers were down. More likely, they were outwitted by whitetails that picked up their scent and worked around the hunters without being seen.

Game biologists have discovered that deer can detect odors a half-mile away; however, the animals will not react to the smell until within 100 yards of its source. It is within this range that countless numbers of hunters, either ignoring the wind or using scents improperly, miss their chance for a trophy buck.

Recognizing that deer have a vastly superior sense of smell, modern hunters are seeking ways to overcome their handicap. This is especially true among bowhunters, because they must get within 30 yards of a deer. A number of highly-effective scents are now being marketed and in addition, many hunters are beginning to produce their own.

To get on more equal terms with deer, your first step should be to eliminate as many man-related scents as possible. Before you take off on a hunt, think about what you are taking into the woods that is a foreign odor to deer.

I used to spend one week each fall hunting in the mountains of east Tennessee. One of my partners thought it was the mark of Daniel Boone not to bathe for the entire week. After a day or two of climbing those steep mountains, he would complain of not seeing any deer, while everyone else was spotting animals. He also complained because no one would let him sleep in their tent. We do have an odor and the serious hunter should consider a daily bath, using odor-free soap. With human odors reduced as much as possible, your next step is to decide which type of scent to use.

While some manufacturers claim differently, most scents fall into two categories: masking and attracting. Masking scents cover up the human odor. Attracting scents, or *lures*, draw bucks during the rut.

For the past five years, I have been conducting my own research on masking scents and lures on lands in southwestern Alabama. These lands cater to bowhunters and gun hunters from mid-October through January, a long enough period for studying scents under a variety of conditions. My findings have been interesting and enlightening. Here is a summary of what I have observed.

## Masking Scents

Using scents to mask human odor improves the hunter's odds, no matter which type of hunting technique he prefers. The

*Today's hunter can choose from a wide array of scents and lures, including turpentine for hunting in pine woodlands.*

key to using a masking scent, I have found, is to select a scent that deer are accustomed to. For instance, one year a hunter from Florida used an apple scent, then chose a tree stand on the edge of a cornfield. Another hunter from Oklahoma chose a tree stand at the opposite end of the field. He used skunk scent. We observed deer moving around the Florida hunter at a safe distance. The Oklahoma hunter shot his buck at short range. There were no apple trees in the area, so the apple odor was foreign to deer. But skunks are plentiful and the deer paid little attention to this familiar odor. The obvious lesson is that before you use commercial scents, make sure the scents occur naturally in your hunting area.

Bobcat urine is one of the most successful masking scents I have used. A smelly scent, it can be purchased from most sporting goods stores. During one bow season, I had to cross an oat field twice to get to my tree stand on the far edge of the field. I had put bobcat urine on my boots before leaving the truck. Two hours after I settled into my stand, I watched five bucks and four does feeding in the field, passing back and forth across my trail. They showed no concern.

I find it interesting that biologists have discovered that deer are attracted to the scent of certain predators, including bobcats. The reason is not known, but sometimes deer will follow the scent of a predator to its source.

A variety of masking scents are free for the taking. Two popular, wild-growing scents include pine needles and a weed commonly called rabbit tobacco (*Gnaphalium obtusifolium*). To use the pine needle scent, simply pull off a handful of fresh needles, break and rub them between your palms, then wipe the juice on your hunting clothes. Leaves from cedar trees also work well.

Using rabbit tobacco was a trick used by the early mountain men. They would gather a handful of the leaves, crush and wad them into a tight ball, then place the strong-smelling plant in their coat pocket or hat brim. Deer are accustomed to the smell of rabbit tobacco. You can find the plant along dry, open areas such as old fields, logging roads, and abandoned homesites. The plant stands from one to three feet high and has narrow leaves that are dark green on top and silvery-gray underneath. Look for its white to cream-colored flowers from August to October. Rabbit tobacco is also called poverty weed, old field balsam, cudweed, and cat foot in various parts of North America.

When hunting in apple country, you can cut an apple in half

and rub the juicy side on your pants. A better method is to put some pure cider in a small plastic squirt bottle. Apply the scent to your pants and the trees around your stand.

When hunting around dairy or beef cattle farms, a good scent to consider is that of cattle. Deer that share the feed and salt of livestock are familiar with their smell. The scent is not available commercially, but there are ways to impart it to your clothes. You could hang your clothes in a barn overnight or, as some dedicated bowhunters do, you could walk through fresh cow manure, working it into the crevices of your boots or smearing it on your trouser legs. The latter method can make a warm afternoon on a tree stand interesting.

One of the most successful bowhunters was Ben Rodgers Lee of wild turkey hunting fame. When preparing to hunt deer in pine woodlands, he washed his hunting clothes in pine-scented disinfectants. These products are used around the home for cleaning cabinets and washing garbage pails, but can also be used for laundry. They contain a high percentage of pine oil, which leaves the clothes smelling like the piney woods. Ben took a number of whitetails with his bow each year, so it must work.

*On this outing, the author wears cedar-based cover scent because of the abundance of cedar trees.*

*Apply cover scents before entering the woods. Sprinkle several drops on your trousers (left) and on your boots (right). Some hunters strap scent pads to their boots.*

Another good masking scent when hunting in pines is turpentine. This is a pure product of the pine tree and a few drops on your boots and pants should do the job. Be careful not to use too much; it is a strong scent and using too much could make deer cautious.

Apply your masking scent before you begin your hunt. The most effective way is to sprinkle a few drops on each boot and also around the bottom of your trousers.

To get the most from your cover scent, you should be aware of some facts. First, regardless of how good your scent may be, you still must hunt with the wind in your favor. Even the best cover scent won't hide all human odors. Second, understand that masking scents are an aid to hunting success, not a shortcut. You still must use other skills and proven techniques. Third, many hunters think that if a little cover scent is good, a lot will be great. However, too much has the reverse effect on whitetails and alarms them. In short, the value of masking scents, when used according to instructions, is to simply help you operate in a deer's territory without having his radar-like nose detect your presence.

### Attracting Scents

Attractor or lure scents consist of deer urine. They are effective during the rut when bucks are using their keen sense of smell to locate does. Scrape hunting (page 57) is a relatively new technique that makes good use of lure scents. Those who have learned the finer points of scrape hunting are producing some excellent bucks. Most experts, including manufacturers of deer scents, agree that buck lures should only be used during the rut; using them at other times may alarm deer.

**Storing Scents**

Manufacturers tell me that many hunters ruin the effectiveness of their scents by not properly storing the product. Keep the bottle in a cool, shaded location with the cap tight. When exposed to air for long periods of time, many scents and lures lose their strength. Also, placing them in a hot area or in the sun will weaken the scent. Avoid tossing a bottle of cover scent onto the dashboard and leaving it for a long period.

As we continue to research this fascinating subject, we will no doubt find that not everything works every time for everyone. But more often than not, masking scents and attractors can improve your chances of bringing home some venison.

# 19

# How to Stay Warm
# While Hunting

It was a typical late November deer hunt in the South. The thermometer hovered around 30 degrees and a damp wind was gusting up to 15 miles per hour. Fred had been sitting on his metal tree stand since daybreak. Shivering, he traded his bow from one hand to the other, plunging the free hand into his jacket pocket for warmth. He had on boxer shorts, a T-shirt, blue jeans, a cotton flannel shirt, an Army field jacket, cotton socks, and tennis shoes. Pulling an almost numb hand out of his pocket, he scratched his bare head and wondered why anybody would hunt when they were so miserable.

The question I'm asked more than any other is: "How can I stay warm in the woods while deer hunting?" To learn how to stay warm, we must first understand our source of body heat and how we lose it.

Humans, like all mammals, are *homoiotherms*, which means we must maintain a stable body temperature. When away from external sources of heat, our only heat source is that which we produce internally. This inner warmth primarily comes from burning food, or the oxidation of carbohydrates.

Carbohydrates, our major source of warmth, are easily digested and provide fast energy for muscles, nerves, and brain. The body does not store them for future use, because they are burned within a short period of time and must be replenished often if we are to stay warm. Carbohydrates are available to us in the form of raisins, chocolate, candy, sugar, and fruits.

On a cold day afield, you may lose body heat in any of five different ways: conduction, radiation, convection, evaporation, and respiration. We have very little control over heat loss through *respiration.* The air we breathe enters cold and leaves warm. The only way we could control this loss would be to quit breathing. But we can control other forms of heat loss.

You recall at the beginning of this chapter, Fred was sitting on a metal tree stand holding a bow in his bare hand. Both objects were cold and Fred was losing heat by *conduction.* If Fred's clothing got wet due to sweating while he walked into the woods, he would lose more heat by conduction, because the cold, wet clothing was touching his flesh.

Also, we noticed that Fred was not wearing a hat. The head is the only part of the body where blood vessels do not constrict to conserve heat, because they must supply the brain with oxygen to insure its proper functioning. Winter survival experts estimate that 50 percent of the body's total heat production may be lost through an unprotected head. This form of heat loss is known as *radiation.*

Fred's entire outfit was made up of cotton and synthetic garments. There wasn't anything to stop the cold air from washing away his warmth. The movement of air around his body created a wind-chill factor that pulled body surface warmth away and replaced it with cold air faster than the body could rewarm it. This heat loss is known as *convection.*

If Fred did much walking to get into the woods and if he exerted much effort in putting up his tree stand and climbing into it, chances are his light clothing was damp with sweat. Fred lost heat by *evaporation.*

While evaporation is the natural way the body cools itself, sweating is very dangerous during cold weather. Improperly dressed, as Fred was, the clothing around his body absorbed moisture. This moisture moves through the layers of clothing until it reaches a layer that is below dew point temperature. Here, it condenses and wets the layer. Then the moisture wicks back to the skin. Sweat-soaked clothing causes rapid chilling of the skin. There is a big difference between the healthy sweating of a long day of bass fishing and the sweat of winter which can lead to chills, frostbite, and hypothermia.

No wonder Fred was cold. He was not prepared for cold-weather hunting, and because he wasn't, he spent a day trying to stay warm. He wasted a day's hunting opportunity.

**Clothing for Cold-weather Hunting**

The best way to dress for a cold day in the field is to wear clothing that preserves your body heat while allowing body moisture to evaporate freely. This is accomplished through *layering*, or wearing alternate layers of clothing to provide insulation and ventilation.

The first layer is underwear. Since it is worn closest to the skin, it should "breathe," allowing moisture to escape. If you must walk to your stand or if you are stalk hunting, then chances are, you will work up a sweat.

The first rule to keeping warm is to stay dry. I like to wear underwear made from a synthetic, long-chain polymer fiber, called polypropylene. This fiber will not absorb moisture, but will re-

*Refueling your body's furnace helps you to stay warm on a deer stand.*

move moisture from your skin. I have tried this underwear in a variety of cold, damp conditions and found it to be the warmest. Even on the coldest days of the deer season I stay warm.

The second layer should include a wool shirt and trousers. Wool has been overlooked for many years, especially in the South, as an insulating material. However, it insulates better than any other fiber when wet.

Many hunters wear a belt secured tightly around their waist to hold up their trousers. This restricts circulation and stops ventilation. Instead, get a pair of suspenders and keep your pants loose around the waist. Hunters in colder climates have been doing this for centuries.

One company, Elastic Products Division in North Carolina, has developed a heavy-duty, extra-wide suspender that is designed for the hunter and is available in hunter orange.

The third layer should be a jacket of wool or a coat filled with Thinsulate, Quallofil, down, Dacron II, or Polar Guard. Each of these fillers has its weak and strong points. You should have some idea as to the type of terrain and weather conditions in which you will be hunting. This is important when selecting the filler material. If you hunt different types of game, you may want to consider a reversible coat that has blaze orange on one side and a camouflage pattern on the other. Manufacturers are building flexibility into coats now that zip apart from liners and vests to fit the conditions.

The fourth and final layer to consider is a rain suit. Wetness can be deadly in the backcountry, so keep a high-quality rain outfit handy.

One of the most important items you can wear is a cap or hat. I prefer a camouflage wool stocking cap in cold weather. If I get caught out in a cold wind or rain, I use the waterproof hood of my rain suit jacket. Not only does it keep out moisture, it's also an excellent wind-breaker.

Wool mittens work best for keeping your hands warm, but under hunting conditions they may not be practical. The next best hand protectors are wool gloves with a wind-proof shell. If you anticipate wet conditions, keep an extra pair of wool gloves in the pocket of your hunting coat.

Our feet get coldest the fastest. This is not without good reason. Our body is programmed to automatically regulate its warmth requirements for survival. When the core temperature drops slightly, the body adjusts heat production, and circulation

*This hunter wears clothes in layers and protects his head with a warm stocking cap and face mask. He will remain warm, despite frigid conditions.*

to the extremities is curtailed. The feet, being the farthest from the core, are the first to feel the reduced circulation. This explains why a hat can help keep your feet warm.

Assuming that your hat is on and your body is properly wrapped in layers, there is little reason for your feet to get cold, provided they are adequately covered. Start with two pairs of wool socks. Since your feet sweat easily, wool works best because it insulates when wet. If wool irritates your skin, start with a thin pair of silk or nylon socks. You may want to wear only one pair of wool socks if the weather is not too cold.

Before you put on your boots, carefully eliminate all wrinkles in your socks. Wrinkles slow down blood circulation to the feet and toes. Always carry an extra pair of wool socks, especially if you do a lot of walking. Change socks if your feet become wet and cold.

Be sure to keep your boots water repellent. Do not lace them too tightly, cutting circulation and causing cold feet.

If you are properly covered and you still have cold feet, check the following: Are your feet wet? Are the clothes on your legs too tight or, if you are on a stand, is the way you are sitting cutting off circulation in your legs?

Now that we are dressed correctly, how can we stay warm under hunting conditions that involve alternately walking and sitting? The first rule is to avoid sweating. As mentioned, your winter apparel should be loose fitting, which creates a bellows action that forces moisture out around your neck. As you walk, maintain a slow pace and avoid working up a heavy sweat. If you get too warm, take the following action in order: 1) Take off your gloves, 2) unzip your jacket, 3) remove your hat, 4) take off your jacket. When you sit down, begin putting the items back on as you cool off. Once you get accustomed to maintaining constant warmth without sweating, you will be amazed at how comfortable you can stay on a cold day.

As we pointed out in the beginning of this article, carbohydrates are the inner source of our warmth. Since this "fuel" cannot be stored, it is necessary to replenish your system during a cold day's hunt. Keep a few high-energy food bars, or *nonmelting* chocolate candy in you hunting coat pocket or day pack. Nibble these foods throughout the day. You will be keeping fuel in the body's furnace.

Hunters who backpack or camp during cold weather should never sleep in their clothes. As you sleep, your body renews its energy supply, giving off a lot of moisture. This moisture is absorbed by your clothes, so in the morning, they will be damp. This is why many seasoned outdoorsmen sleep in the nude and air out their sleeping bag daily. Without this airing, the sleeping bag will stay damp and cold.

Cold-weather hunting can be dangerous to those who have not taken the time to learn the art of staying warm. Hypothermia kills hunters every year. But, if for no other reason than skilled hunting, you should learn to stay warm.

Fred didn't enjoy his hunt. Regardless if he was a good or bad hunter, his thoughts and efforts were turned to staying warm, not hunting.

Learn how to stay warm, then hunt on the cold days. There will be fewer hunters, no snakes and insects, and you will have the satisfaction of knowing that you have come one step closer to being a master outdoorsman.

# 20

# The Day Pack &
# Survival Kit

A lmost every survey that has been conducted to determine why modern man hunts, comes up with "the pleasure of being afield" as the number one answer. Yet, how many hunters truly "go afield"—that is, out of sight of the nearest road?

Wildlife managers and conservation officers cite three major reasons why many hunters never venture very far: They need to return to the car for a coffee break and lunch, they fear a sudden change in weather, and they are fearful of getting lost.

A day pack and survival kit, combined or used separately, can eliminate many of the reasons for not penetrating the back-country for a full day. When you consider that game is often more plentiful and hunters considerably fewer in off-road areas, isn't it worth the slight addition to your hunting gear?

In addition, the new-found confidence and independence that comes with the day pack and survival kit will make your hunting more comfortable. You will be able to spend more time afield and less time thinking about being lost or needing to return to your vehicle.

### Day Pack

My day pack is blaze orange in color and small in size. It is constructed of coated nylon pack cloth, has one large inside pocket and two outside pockets, comes with padded shoulder

**A day pack and its contents will enable a hunter to stay on his tree stand throughout the day.**

straps, stores easily, and is inexpensive (less than $20). When bowhunting, I switch to a camouflage day pack.

The items you carry in your day pack depend on your personal needs and taste, and the type of game you pursue. The pack can also include various survival items. Following are the items I carry in my pack for a day of deer hunting—use my list as a suggested guide for selecting your own equipment.

• Since much deer hunting is done by stalk hunting, an extra pair of wool socks is a welcome item at midday. A change also helps during wet weather.

• The safest and easiest way to get a deer out of the woods is with a drag rope. The rope can also be used for getting equipment in and out of a tree stand. As a survival tool, it is invaluable for shelter construction.

• An extra pair of shooting gloves can make a long stand more bearable on a cold day.

• A clear vinyl rain suit can spell comfort during a rain storm or cold wind. The transparent suit allows your blaze orange coat or jacket to show through.

• A small camera can capture many fun moments afield. Photos of hunting friends and their trophies are a great way to relive memorable hunts.

• Take along a flashlight. It can help you get to your stand earlier and bring you out later. I feel safer walking in the woods before daylight than I do walking in after daylight. Most hunters know that deer don't carry flashlights. Also, the flashlight is a good signaling device should you become lost.

• Toilet tissue serves several purposes. The first is obvious. It is also a good fire starter. When trailing a wounded deer, you can drop small pieces of tissue by each blood sign. This makes it easier to stay on the trail, not to mention finding your way back out. Many hunters concentrate on trailing wounded game and forget how to get back. The toilet tissue trail will bring you back.

• A canteen of water or insulated bottle of coffee can save a trip back to the car and make a full day on the stand more enjoyable.

• Binoculars are a must for deer hunting.

• Always carry a U.S.G.S. topographic map of your area.

• A sportsman's signal kit meets many of the signaling needs of a lost hunter. It contains two aerial flares, an orange smoke signal, fire starter kit, and signal mirror.

• A first aid kit can be as small or as large as you think

necessary. The trail kit shown is lightweight and includes water purification tablets.

• Extra ammunition can be carried quietly in the day pack. Leave your cartridges in their original Styrofoam or plastic containers.

• A bright red distress marker takes little room, and aside from being an excellent ground-to-air marker, it can be used to make an emergency shelter.

• Waterproof matches should be carried in the pack and on the person.

• A police whistle makes a good signaling device because it carries farther and lasts longer than the human voice.

• The Wallet Survival Guide is a comprehensive survival manual; it is available at sport shops and is a good addition to your pack.

*Day pack items include: (1) pack, (2) extra wool socks, (3) drag rope, (4) extra shooting gloves, (5) rain suit, (6) small camera, (7) flashlight, (8) toilet tissue, (9) canteen, (10) binoculars, (11) topo map, (12) signal kit, (13) first aid kit, (14) extra ammunition, (15) distress marker, (16) waterproof matches, (17) police whistle, (18) survival guide, (19) cover scent or lure, (20) knife sharpening stone, (21, 22, 23) high-energy foods, (24) extra boot laces.*

• Cover scent or lure is used to mask your scent and to work buck scrapes.

• A knife sharpening stone helps.

• You may select high-energy trail foods or a lunch you prepared. Just keep a little aside for that day when you get turned around.

• Extra boot laces.

Most survival experts and guides suggest that even though you carry a well-equipped day pack or survival kit, you should also carry a knife, waterproof matches, map, compass, whistle, and space blanket on your person. These survival basics will see you through if you should become separated from your pack or kit.

My day pack with the above items weighs 14 pounds. Your choice of items may run the weight up or down, depending upon your needs.

**Survival Kit**

A survival kit can be used with your day pack to give you an edge on almost any unexpected event. If you leave the tree stand to trail game or explore another area, take the small survival kit along and leave the day pack at your stand. If you should become lost, you are prepared.

Many hunters do not want to have the comforts and extra weight of a day pack, but they do want the assurance of a complete survival kit, one that has the items necessary for making shelter, signaling, building a fire, securing food, purifying water, navigating, and providing simple first aid.

According to the National Rifle Association, a hunter in a survival crisis is generally faced with a short term situation—usually less than three days. Searches can take time, however, and the lost hunter should plan for the worst, conserve energy, and improve existing conditions. He should stay in one location, assisting searchers through visual and audible signaling. This includes ground-to-air signals which all hunters should know.

It is with these needs in mind that the following survival kit was developed:

• The kit bag is an Army surplus individual first aid pouch. It is sturdy and fits on the belt easily. Its small size allows it to fit in a day pack, backpack, vehicle glove box or tacklebox.

• The blaze orange smoke signal, available from most camping suppliers, is an excellent daytime signaling device to use in

*Survival kit should be com-
pact enough to carry with
ease.*

conjunction with ground-to-air signals.

• The wire saw, which coils up to store easily, can be used to cut poles for shelter, wood for fire, or for helping to quarter large game.

• Many survival stories are told of hunters who made it to a pay phone but had no change. Carry enough change for a call.

• A coil of 20-pound test fishing line can be used for making shelter, mending clothes, and making snares, as well as for fishing.

• The space emergency blanket folds to the size of a cigarette pack. It can be made into a lean-to or used as a blanket that reflects up to 90 percent of your body's heat.

• Aspirin to ease pain.

• Band-aids.

• Police whistle for signaling.

• A candle stub for starting a fire.

• A Scout-type pocket knife.

• Antiseptic for scratches and wounds.

• The signal mirror can be spotted for miles by search planes and forest fire towers.

• Beef broth has some food value and makes wild food dishes taste much better.

• The Wallet Survival Guide is a small, but complete survival manual.

• Waterproof matches.

• Water purification tablets.

• A small tackle box can be made by taking a plastic bottle and winding several feet of six-pound test fishing line around it. Hold the line in place with tape. In the bottle, place several small hooks, split-shot, a small bluegill popping bug, and a small dry fly. Think small, as it is usually easier to catch small fish. (The food requirement during survival situations is less than most people think.)

*Survival kit items include: (1) Army surplus first aid pouch, (2) smoke signal, (3) wire saw, (4) coins, (5) fishing line, (6) space blanket, (7) aspirin, (8) band-aids, (9) police whistle, (10) candle, (11) pocket knife, (12) antiseptic, (13) signal mirror, (14) beef broth, (15) survival guide, (16) waterproof matches, (17) water purification tablets, (18) small tackle box, (19) tweezers, (20) lip protection, (21) metal match, (22) steel wool, (23) back-up compass.*

- Tweezers for removing splinters, etc.
- Lip protection from wind and sun.
- Metal match which can be used as a back-up fire starter.
- Size 000 steel wool for igniting tinder. One spark from the metal match in the loose steel wool produces a hot glow that will start dry tinder. Steel wool works even when wet.
- A back-up compass. Carry the other compass on your person.

You can find smaller, as well as much larger survival kits, but this one will serve most of your needs. An addition for the hunter in snow country is a collapsible aluminum cup or a folded piece of aluminum foil for melting snow for water.

Even with your survival kit, don't neglect to learn survival skills such as how to signal, and how to use your map and compass. A hunter with a survival kit full of items he doesn't know how to use, can be a hunter in trouble.

# 21

# The Skills to Survive

The afternoon had started out as a typical squirrel hunt. Three of us, all students at Auburn University, had taken an afternoon off to bag a few squirrels in the big hardwoods of nearby Tuskegee National Forest. As dusk gave way to darkness, two of us sat on the fender of the car reliving the accounts of our afternoon hunt. Suddenly it dawned on us that the third member of our party was taking a long time to return. Yet we didn't worry, because Mike was a highly-trained and experienced hunter. He was working on his master's degree in forest management and had just recently returned from four years in the Alaskan backcountry.

After waiting another 30 minutes, I blew the car horn three times. No response. For the next 10 minutes, we blew the horn and shouted, stopping occasionally to listen. It was becoming very clear that Mike was in trouble. We began to ask questions like, had he shot himself accidentally or could he have had a heart attack? Mike was a believer in hunter safety and was in excellent physical condition, so these questions seemed out of place. The reality that Mike was lost began to sink in. Shortly thereafter, an organized search began.

An hour after midnight, a wild-looking man broke through a thicket and ran into the beam of a searcher's spotlight. Mike was wide-eyed and confused. His clothing from the waist down was torn to shreds, and his legs and arms were bloody from hundreds of scratches. The .22 rifle, hunting coat and cap he had taken into the woods were gone, where he did not know. Later we learned that his hunting coat contained matches, extra ammunition, a pocket knife, and three squirrels.

It took Mike two weeks to fully recover from his brief, but brutal ordeal. He recalled the panic that struck him at dark when he realized he was lost. He remembered running for long periods of time. He also remembered a feeling of fear toward the strange people shouting and flashing lights in the woods. The feelings of embarrassment, guilt, confusion, and exhaustion all raced through his mind at the same time. Mike, an above-average hunter and outdoorsman, had come face-to-face with a survival situation and had failed to use his outdoor skills.

Each year, hundreds of hunters are suddenly shocked into the reality that even they can get lost, stranded, weathered in, or immobilized by injury. At that point, they must put their survival skills to work. If they have taken the time to learn these skills and to prepare themselves for the unexpected, their situation will be one of adventure and challenge, rather than an ordeal or perhaps tragedy.

The first step toward survival is to always let someone know where you are going in the backcountry and when you expect to return. If you get into trouble, authorities will soon know it and begin their search in the right location.

Let's assume it is a nice fall day and you have walked two miles into the woods to bowhunt in a remote swamp. Late in the afternoon, it begins to cloud up, so you decide to head for the car. On the way out, you lose the trail and suddenly realize you are lost. Night is rapidly approaching. What should you do?

## Stay Calm and Think

Your first survival skill is the ability to admit you are lost. With this accepted, stop, sit down, and think. Convince yourself to avoid panic and to stay calm. Accept the challenge and prepare to make the best of your adventure. If you informed friends or family where you were going and when you planned to return, chances are, someone will begin looking for you soon after dark. In fact, most lost people are found within a few hours after they are reported missing. Even in the more remote areas of the U.S., 99 percent of the lost people are found within 72 hours.

Once you have gotten over the initial shock that you are lost, look around and evaluate your situation.

*Airborne search parties have a better chance of spotting a white shirt or even bare skin if you move into a clearing in the woods.*

**Signaling**

Since people will be looking for you soon, your first concern should be preparing to let people know where you are. In our assumed situation, as in most cases, a fire is the best signal device. At night, it can be seen for miles from the air and a fair distance on the ground. During the day, the smoke can be seen from the air as well as from forest fire towers which overlook most woodlands. Not only does a fire serve as a good signal, it also keeps you warm, gives you a somewhat reassuring feeling, and can be used for cooking if you happen to have food with you. More about fires later.

Other signal devices to consider include a whistle that can be heard much farther than the human voice and will last long after a shouting person becomes hoarse. A small mirror or shiny object can be seen for miles by an airplane during the day. Also, a plane can spot a blaze orange vest, white T-shirt, or even light-colored skin if the lost person is in an open area. Other signaling devices include small aerial flares for nighttime use and blaze orange smoke signals for daytime. These handy devices may be obtained from backpack and sporting goods stores, or ordered from outdoor catalog houses.

If all else fails, locate an opening in the woods and make a large "X" with logs, rocks, or whatever is available. All airplane pilots know the "X" as a signal for help.

Any combination of these signals or if available, using all of them, is a good strategy for being found.

A word of caution: many survival books suggest firing three shots evenly distributed as a lost signal. It doesn't work. During hunting season, three shots are heard all the time. Several years ago, I was hunting with the editor of a well-known outdoor magazine when he got his four-wheel-drive vehicle hopelessly stuck far back in the woods. Several times, he fired thee-shot volleys, but no one in our party paid any attention. After a long, cold walk, he told us in person about his problem. The only time three shots might work is when you know a search party is in the area. Then, it could have some benefit; otherwise, three shots to an unknowing world are meaningless and a waste of ammunition which might be needed for food-gathering.

**To Build a Fire**

Let's return to our predicament. We realize we are lost, we have calmed down, and have wisely decided to wait for rescue.

*The "X" and mirror make excellent signals.*

Next, we should try to find an opening in the woods where our signals can be seen from the air. If you can see an opening, get to it. If you cannot see an opening, search for one within a radius of about 200 yards—but *do not* search any farther than that.

Once in an opening, we can take out our waterproof match container and build a fire. Sounds easy, doesn't it? But what if you don't have matches? And what if you don't know how to build a fire? The unknowing person might say you can always build a fire with flint and steel, or by making a fire drill. Wrong!

Except for a few experts, there are few among us who can start a fire without matches. Despite what many survival books say, there is no substitute for dry matches. Make it a practice to carry a water-proof match container at all times.

With this taken care of, let's get down to another common misconception—that most outdoorsmen even with matches can build a fire. Recently, I was talking with a veteran search and rescue official who pointed out that each year, he finds many lost outdoorsmen who are cold and without fire. "They had matches

*Waterproof containers for matches include (left to right): commercially-made plastic (with whistle) and metal containers, and plastic film cannister.*

in most cases," he told me. "But they used them up just trying to get a fire started."

Take the time to learn an old Boy Scout skill: how to build a fire with just one match. Learn what makes good tinder, such as a bird nest, bark from a birch tree, a knot or knob from a pine tree (called a *pine lighter* by woodsmen), or cedar bark. Don't assume you know any of this. Go out and find these items, then use them to build a fire. In a damp situation, don't forget that dead standing wood and limbs are usually drier than pieces lying on the ground. The dead lower branches of evergreen trees make ideal tinder because they contain resin, which burns readily. Become a fire-building expert—it may save your life.

### Shelter

Now that we have a fire going, what's next? You recall that when we got lost, night was approaching and it was cloudy. Our next consideration should be shelter. If it were a cold winter's evening, shelter would be a must. The easiest to make is a lean-to, especially if you have a small space blanket. If you don't have a space blanket, consider roofing your lean-to with pine boughs, loose bark, or whatever you can find. Use your imagination. To keep your mind occupied and off your dilemma, see how good a shelter you can make.

I recall fondly one hunter I helped to find several years ago. He had been lost for two days, and when we found him, he was resting comfortably in what seemed like a small homestead. His camp was so cozy that we stayed there overnight. On the way out the next morning, he said that he had actually enjoyed the experience and planned to intentionally get lost again.

Other impromptu shelters can be made from blown-down trees, your canoe, or rock overhangs. Use due caution with fire and don't camp with a den of rattlesnakes. Common sense and a little ingenuity can do a lot to build an adequate shelter.

**Food and Water**

Many outdoorsmen think that food and water are your most important needs in a survival situation. Far from it. It has been proven many times that most people can live three days without water and easily three weeks or more without food. So don't panic and think you are going to die from lack of food or water the first night. Odds are great that you will be found long before you need either one.

*Lost hunters should stay put. Build a shelter and fire, then relax and wait to be found. Most hunters are rescued within 72 hours.*

While there are various ways to locate water, your best bet is to carry it in your day pack. This is especially true when hunting in arid regions. In fact, when I'm hunting in a dry area, I carry two canteens. It's a little extra weight, but it is good insurance against dehydration if I should get stranded or lost.

However, if it is of any comfort, most areas in North America usually have some source of water that you can find.

I also make it a point to keep some jerky, candy bars, and granola in my day pack for emergency purposes. I have been stranded for several days at a time, and while I was in no danger of starving to death, the goodies made my ordeal much less painful. In a survival situation, the hunter is armed with the means of taking animals for food and with a little luck, should not face any danger from starvation.

# 22

# Managing
# White-tailed Deer

A nyone who hunts whitetails should have some idea of what is involved in managing the animal. In the early 1900s, the deer herd throughout the United States was in trouble. The population had declined to an all-time low, and in many areas whitetails had completely vanished.

Thanks to modern wildlife management techniques and programs—many supported by funds derived from license fees and special taxes that hunters imposed upon themselves—we now have a record number of whitetails.

The basic approach in deer management is to treat the species as a renewable resource. Biologists strive to keep deer herds in balance with the amount and quality of available habitat. The only practical way to control deer numbers is by sport hunting—using carefully regulated seasons to harvest a certain number of bucks and does.

It is biologically feasible to harvest whitetails on an annual basis as long as the total number of deer taken does not exceed the number born. Biologists have determined that from 20 to 30 percent of the deer can be removed each year without damaging a healthy herd. Declining populations, however, usually require a reduced harvest, depending upon management goals.

Every deer range, whether it be the river bottoms of Montana or the swamps of Florida, can produce only a certain amount

*A given unit of land can support only a given number of whitetails. When deer become too abundant, they can seriously damage the existing vegetation. Once food is in short supply, the population is likely to crash.*

of deer food per acre. And this food can sustain only a limited number of whitetails. The maximum number of deer that the habitat can support without damage to the vegetation is known as the *carrying capacity.*

If there are fewer deer than available food, the herd will usually be in excellent condition, because all are well fed. When deer exceed the carrying capacity, what is commonly known as over-population, the same amount of food must be shared by more deer. On the average, the herd will be undernourished. It is a simple matter of dividing up the food. When there is not enough food to go around, natural mortality factors begin to take a heavy toll.

Too little food not only results in weight loss, it also means that deer are not getting enough vitamins, minerals, and other essential elements. Too little Vitamin A, for instance, makes the deer's body more vulnerable to infection and to parasites, like ticks. If Vitamin K is deficient, the deer's system will produce fewer blood coagulants, which also makes the animal more susceptible to parasites. To make matters worse, the deer's body will not produce sufficient antibodies to prevent infectious organisms from entering wounds.

Let's take a look at a newly-established, under-hunted deer herd. Since the herd is just getting started, the number of whitetails is well below what the range can support. This carrying capacity may vary from year to year, depending upon the area's climate, water supply, soil types and their fertility.

For the first few years, the number of deer remains below the carrying capacity. In this new herd, food is plentiful and all animals are generally in good health. They have a few parasites, but are not bothered by them. Mature bucks grow heavy-beamed antlers with numerous tines and most yearlings have forked antlers. A few have only spikes, but at least the spikes are long. Virtualiy all adult does carry twin fawns or triplets, most of which survive after birth. Many of the yearling does are also pregnant. Because reproduction rates and fawn survival are high, the herd has many relatively young deer.

If the herd continues to grow and hunting is non-existent, the total deer population will soon reach the carrying capacity and there will not be enough nourishment to go around. The malnourished does may live through the winter, but many will be so weakened that their fawns do not survive. Those does that give birth will probably have just a single fawn. Bucks continue to breed, but their racks are smaller. The antlers, if any, of yearlings are predominantly spikes, many only two to three inches long.

*Sound wildlife management can produce whitetail trophies such as these on a continuing basis.*

As the herd continues to increase and malnutrition becomes prevalent, some 2½-year-old bucks produce only spikes. Genetics plays an important role in the potential development and size of a buck's antlers, but a hungry buck will never produce a large rack, regardless of his genetic background.

Deer numbers will continue to increase beyond the carrying capacity, because reproduction never ceases entirely. The animals must eat, and the most preferred and nutritious food plants become heavily browsed. Once this happens, deer shift to less preferred foods. Since the most nutritious plants may actually be eliminated, the carrying capacity may shrink as the herd increases.

Often we see this situation in areas that are under-hunted, or where a bucks-only rule is in effect. In these cases, many hunters believe that spikes should not be harvested, so there will be more trophy deer in future years. This is one of many fallacies surrounding deer management. Those who advocate this theory do not realize that antler development depends on both heredity and food.

Some deer, regardless of age or the abundance of food, always have unbranched antlers. If these deer are protected, while those with massive racks are harvested, we could end up with a herd containing an extremely large number of bucks that will never have anything but spikes. Until the deer population is reduced to the point that each individual has ample food year-round, body weight and antler development will continue to decline.

Some hunters are fearful that harvesting antlerless deer will result in overkill. The probability of this happening is very slight. Under good conditions, a deer population can more than double itself in two to three years, and the problem of overkill can usually be corrected by reducing the harvest for this period.

The number of deer to harvest in a particular area is determined by closely monitoring the herd's condition along with population trends. Biologists collect data at check stations during hunting season by aging and weighing harvested animals, collecting stomachs to determine internal parasite loads, measuring antlers, and examining reproductive tracts. They also conduct numerous surveys throughout the year to estimate deer numbers, population trends, sex ratios, number of fawns produced per doe, and winter mortality. These and other data are used to evaluate the condition of the deer herd and to determine its response to hunting and environmental factors. The end results are hunting seasons and bag limits.

*The hunting season is important to wildlife managers because it offers them a chance to collect a large amount of data regarding the age and condition of deer.*

## Private Management Projects

Landowners, hunting clubs, or hunters who want to upgrade deer habitat on private lands would be well-advised to seek the help of a professional wildlife biologist. The wildlife manager can design a management plan specifically for your tract of land. Free consulting service is available from many government agencies, such as the U.S. Fish & Wildlife Service, Soil Conservation Service, Cooperative Extension Service, and state game and fish agencies. Or, you may want to hire a private consultant to draw up a comprehensive plan that integrates wildlife and forest management techniques.

Practices, other than population control, that should be included in a whitetail management plan include:

1) Completely protecting the herd from illegal hunting.

2) Providing year-round protection from dogs.

3) In southeastern states, using prescribed burning in pine-type forests during February and March, and where feasible, on

a two-year rotation basis. In northern ranges, conducting controlled burns or logging projects in aspen and other hardwoods to enhance deer habitat.

4) Limiting clear-cuts to blocks from two to ten acres in size, and not cutting the adjacent tracts for five years. This provides a continuing edge effect, with different age classes of trees, each tract providing a unique variety of food and cover.

5) In timber harvest areas, leaving trees and brushy cover along flowing streams.

6) Planting food plots appropriate to your area. In the Midwest, for example, many landowners leave several rows of corn standing next to good woody cover.

7) Keeping accurate records of each deer harvested, including weight, age, antler measurements, and sex. Have a biologist teach you to age a deer by examining its lower jaw.

Once a management plan is drawn up, everyone involved in the piece of property should follow the plan to the letter. At the end of each year, the wildlife biologist who devised the plan should meet with the group to discuss the harvest data. Together, you can make adjustments to maintain the herd at an optimum level, providing quality hunting for everyone involved.

*Small blocks of clear-cuts provide more edges and a variety of tree age classes. This enables whitetails to find ample food and cover within close proximity of each other.*

23

# Finding & Leasing
# Land for Hunting

George and John had what most deer hunters want—their very own deer lease. They had found a tract of land with plenty of deer sign, located the owner, and after writing him a check, shook hands to formalize their lease.

The night before the bow season found the two anxious hunters setting up camp on their lease. Just after they got the tent up and the fire going, the owner drove up to inform them that he didn't allow camping or fires on his property. They would have to move their camp "right now." Tired and thoroughly disgusted, they struck camp and drove 20 miles to a small town where they checked into a local motel.

Things seemed better the next morning. They got into the woods before daylight and put up their tree stands in a large grove of white oaks. Their short night of moving camp and little sleep seemed worthwhile as they heard the birds awaken, and the first rays of the morning sun sliced through the trees.

Suddenly, they were almost jolted out of their tree stands by two nearby shotgun blasts. Then came a third shot just below their stands. As they climbed down, they were approached by three squirrel hunters. After a short conversation, the bowhunters learned that the other hunters had a squirrel-hunting lease on the same tract. With this disappointment, the hunters went home to wait for the firearms deer season. After all, they were really stalk-hunters and it would be much better next month when the gun season opened. At least they wouldn't have to contend with squirrel hunters.

The opening weekend of gun deer season found George and John stalking quietly on their deer lease. Each had visions of slipping up on old mossy horns. Just after daybreak, they heard what sounded like the howling of wolves along the east border of their lease. Within a few minutes, a dozen hounds ran between the two hunters, hot on the trail of some unseen deer.

The pack of dogs had not been long in passing when the pair heard the music of another pack across the creek that formed the northern boundary of their lease. It was very clear to them that the neighboring landowners weren't stalk hunters. George and John went home, hoping that the "dog drive" hunters on the land surrounding their lease would soon grow tired of hunting and let the woods quiet down.

While waiting for their next hunt, the two lease-holders sold several of their friends a membership in the lease. Since they were all good ol' boys, nobody bothered to set up any rules.

The next Friday found all five of the lease members on the property long before daylight. Some 15 minutes after good daylight, one of the new members got cold, built a fire, and started shouting for John to come join him at the fire. John had been watching a spike trail a doe, but felt compelled to quiet his friend, and put out the roaring bonfire.

Again things got settled and the hunters were at peace with the outdoors. Suddenly there was a shot, then another, another, and several more. One of the new members had gotten bored with the hunt and had started shooting into squirrel nests.

For the next six months, both George and John were in their attorney's office many times trying to straighten out the mess. This nightmare they called a lease almost caused them to swear off deer hunting.

If this deer hunting lease sounds like a horror story, take heed, because it could happen to you. Each year many honorable, well-meaning hunters get mixed up in leases that pose a variety of problems.

Today, the American hunter faces problems his granddaddy never dreamed would arise. Just a few years ago, hunting lands

*Before signing a lease agreement, spend some time walking over the property. You may want to detail the different types of vegetation and terrain, then discuss your findings with a wildlife manager.*

were easily found, most game species were abundant, and landowners were willing to grant permission to almost any asking hunter. But increasing population has changed all this. Our cities are growing, and the fields and forests that were open for hunting are becoming less available. As a result of this land shortage, deer hunters are grouping together to lease deer hunting rights on private land. Properly done, a membership in a deer lease can be one of a hunter's most prized possessions. Improperly done, it can become a nightmare!

**Finding a Good Tract of Land**

The first step in setting up a smooth-working deer lease is to find a good piece of land. Your search should begin in July or August. First, determine the country in which you wish to locate your lease. Next, learn the habits and habitat of the deer in that area. Deer habits, food choices, etc., change with the seasons and from area to area. If you cannot recognize quality habitat, admit it and seek assistance. There are many government agencies in each county with trained personnel who can help you learn to recognize good deer habitat. The Soil Conservation Service, University Extension Service, Game and Fish Division, the U.S. Forest Service—these are just a few that can get you off on the right foot.

As you learn to recognize good deer habitat, sharpen up your skill of reading deer sign. To get a good deer lease, you must be able to recognize whitetail sign like tracks and droppings.

Once you are up-to-date on evaluating the deer habitat and sign, obtain several copies of the county road map.

Set up a series of meeting on a weekday with the following officials: the county agent—he visits all the farms and knows something of the game population, and he knows local landowners who may have a good lease tract; the county forest ranger—he knows the woods; the Soil Conservation Service representative—he is familiar with game management on farms and waterways; and, of course, the local conservation officer. If there is a pulp and paper company or timber company in the county, visit its Woodlands Management office, as many of these timberlands offer excellent deer hunting.

Go alone when visiting these contacts. They talk more openly to one sincere hunter as opposed to a whole group asking many questions at once. Dress casual. Don't look like a Wall Street bank president or an African safari guide. Blend in with the local people.

Years ago, I worked with the Extension Service in Georgia. A group of hunters burst into my office one morning looking for land to lease for deer hunting. They were all wearing cowboy hats, hunting knives, and several had .357 magnums strapped to their sides. Everyone in the office thought Poncho Villa and his gang had arrived. Needless to say, we had a hard time finding them a lease.

Along these same lines, don't take the boss's new Lincoln, as the lease price has a way of going up for pretentious-looking buyers. On the other hand, don't take a sparkling new four-wheel drive with a dozen guns hanging in the window. This seems to advertise to the local people that a safari is looking for a sight to set up its headquarters. Just be yourself.

*Wildlife managers can assist you in obtaining a parcel of land with quality white-tail habitat.*

When you visit each contact, have the official mark on a county road map the areas with good deer populations. Ask him to write down the names and addresses of large landowners in that area. Use a separate map for each contact; you will get more original thoughts by using separate maps.

After completing your visits, compare the maps. Wherever there is an overlap in good deer areas is probably the best hunting in the county.

Your next step will be to ride the roads. As you get to know an area, establish some local contacts. The farmer on the side of the road, the rural mail carrier, and the crossroads store owner are all good people to ask about the local deer situation. Lead into your deer hunting questions slowly. Ask questions such as: "Are deer damaging crops? Are deer a highway hazard? Where do you see deer most often crossing the road?" Mark these areas on your road map.

Once you have marked several hot spots, ride by them. Ask yourself this question: "Is it the right type of habitat?" If so, meet the landowner and discuss the possibilities of leasing, subject to further investigation. Be friendly and don't rush.

**Check Out the Prospective Lease**

Once you have found a willing landowner with a sizable tract of land with a good deer population, you will want to walk the land out thoroughly. Be sure of what you are getting. Check out the following questions, and if you don't get a satisfactory answer, beware.

• Does the deer sign and habitat indicate that the land has a good deer population and is capable of keeping it?

• Are the boundaries well marked? If not, who will mark them? This is necessary to keep you and your members on the lease, and others off.

• Is the land large enough for your group? A good rule of thumb is no less than 50 acres per hunter.

• Is the landowner willing to perform game management practices such as prescribed burning, planting food plots, etc., or will he permit your group to carry out recommended practices?

• Will the landowner lease all hunting rights and make sure that only your group hunts the land? Do not get involved in a tract of land if there is a different group hunting each species. Insist on and be willing to pay for total hunting rights.

• Are there any conflicting land uses anticipated for the tract? It is hard to hunt deer when a strip mine suddenly shows up on your lease or half the land is clear-cut and planted in pasture.

• Do the neighboring landowners hunt the way you do? Dog hunters fit well with dog hunters, stand hunters with stand hunters, but mix them and unhappiness can be the end product. A lease is worthless if you spend all your time feuding with the adjacent landowners or hunters.

• Does your type of hunting agree with the landowner? Does he expect shotguns only, when you prefer rifles? Does he want stand hunting and you want dog drives? Clear this ahead of time.

• Who will be responsible for maintenance of roads and gates? A large lease whose roads are washed out is useless to the hunter unwilling to walk long distances. Also, gates have a way of getting knocked down and must be repaired in order to stop trespassers.

• Will the landowner give you camping permission or will he permit you to erect a shelter? Perhaps he has a tenant house, maple sugar shack, or trapper's cabin that he will rent to your group as a camphouse.

*A good lease can provide many years of enjoyable hunting.*

## Get Your Lease in Writing

Once these questions have been answered, determine the cost and the length of the lease. The cost is up to you and the landowner; however, the length of the lease should be from three to five years with an option to renew. A good tract of land, properly managed for deer and leased to a sincere club, will increase in value. The older the lease, the more valuable it usually becomes to the members, so don't settle for one year.

Perhaps the most important part of this chapter is this: Once you reach a full agreement with the landowner, get the lease and all the particulars in writing. Make your lease a legal document. It will solve many potential problems.

## Consider Forming a Club

If more than two or three hunters are involved in the lease, consider forming a club. Better yet, set up a chapter of a national group by writing to the group's headquarters for details. If the tract is large, there is economy in having several members. Also, there is more help in carrying out the chores of maintaining your responsibilities, such as marking boundaries, planting food plots, and repairing the camphouse. If you do set up a club or get several hunters involved, make sure everyone agrees with your method of hunting. Don't mix competing styles of hunting.

While I am not a lawyer, I am advised that since a club is engaged in an activity which has potential liability to third parties or to its members, there are advantages to incorporation. If your lawyer agrees with this advice, have him form the club into a corporation and have the lease made in the name of the corporation.

One of the best reasons for forming a club is to set up rules and regulations for members. Properly drawn up and enforced, these rules assure you of a safe and sane hunt. I know of one club of still-hunters that is so well organized that when a member enters the lease, he marks his hunting area on a large map and no other hunter will go into that area. In five years, they have had no disagreements among members or with the landowner.

These are only a few suggestions for leasing deer hunting land. The lease may be as simple or as complex as your members want to make it.

On the next several pages is a sample lease that can be modified easily to fit various situations.

# HUNTING LEASE

This lease is entered into by and between _____

_____ ,
hereinafter referred to as "Lessor" and _____

_____ ,
hereinafter referred to as "Lessee." By doing so each agrees to
the following provisions:

### 1.

Lessor does hereby lease, for the term and amount as per
provisions #2 and #3, and subject to the reservations and conditions hereinafter set forth, the exclusive right to hunt on the
following described tract of land located in _____
County, _____ (state), and described as follows:

### 2.

This lease shall be for a term of _____
unless sooner terminated pursuant to provisions of this agreement hereinafter set forth. Provided that either Lessor or Lessee may cancel this agreement by giving written notice of its
intent to do so thirty (30) days prior to the date that payment for
the next year of the term here provided is due. In which event,
Lessee shall be relieved of the obligation to pay further lease
payments under the terms hereof and shall deliver possession
of the premises.

### 3.

The consideration for which this lease is granted is an annual cash payment to be paid as follows, to-wit:

$_____ on execution hereof:

$_____ on _____ , 19\_\_\_ ;

$_____ on _____ , 19\_\_\_ ;

$_____ on _____ , 19\_\_\_ ;

$_____ on _____ , 19\_\_\_ ;

4.

Lessee agrees that it will not transfer or assign or sublease in whole or in part this lease.

5.

The Lessee will abide by all county, state, and federal laws regarding hunting. Lessee shall be responsible for the conduct of Lessee's members or guests. Any violation of the laws shall be considered just cause for immediate cancellation of this lease by Lessor, and no proration of the lease payment previously paid shall be made.

6.

Lessee will report all big game killed to the Lessor in order that proper wildlife management programs may be conducted.

7.

Lessee may camp or erect any type structure on this tract only after written approval of Lessor is obtained.

8.

Lessee agrees to take good care of the property and will be responsible for any damage to livestock, fences, trees, roads, or structures.

9.

Lessee agrees to exercise extreme care in order that forest fires be avoided and to aid in the prevention and suppression of any fires encountered on the tract. All forest fires will be reported to the county forest ranger promptly.

10.

Lessee agrees that all property of every kind which may be on the premises during the continuance of this lease, whether same is property of Lessor or Lessee, shall be there at the sole risk of Lessee. Lessor shall not be liable to Lessee or to any other person for any injury, loss or damage regardless of the nature thereof to any person or property on the leased premises. Lessee agrees to indemnify and hold harmless Lessor against any and all liability whatsoever for damages to any person or thing because of personal injury or property damage arising out of or resulting from Lessee's use and enjoyment of the privileges herein granted, whether said personal injury or property damage should result from accident, use of firearms, or otherwise occurring on the leased premises during or connected with any hunting, or any other activity organized or conducted by Lessee, its members, guests, servants or employees. In this connection, it is agreed that one of the terms and conditions under which the above premises is leased is that the Lessee assumes responsibility for the conditions of the premises and for any occurrences which happen thereon, including use of roads or other facilities constructed or maintained by Lessor.

Lessee shall, at Lessee's own expense, carry insurance of minimum limits, for the duration of the lease as follows:

Comprehensive General Liability with minimum limits of $100,000 per person and $300,000 per occurrence for bodily injury and $50,000 for property damage.

Certificates indicating this insurance is in effect and a statement that the insurance carrier will not cancel without giving Lessor 30 days' notice, must be filed with Lessor and shall be subject to Lessor's approval.

## 11.

Lessor reserves and shall have the right of ingress and egress into, over and across the said lands during the term of this lease at any time and for any reason it may deem necessary or desirable. Lessor further reserves the right to build or to grant rights of way over, on or under the leased premises for purpose which Lessor deems necessary.

## 12.

Lessee shall not construct any roads or other improvements or make alterations on said lands without prior written consent of Lessor.

## 13.

Lessor reserves the right to deny access to the leased premises to any person or persons for any of the following reasons: carelessness with guns, violations of game laws, trespassing on property of adjoining landowners, acts which could reasonably be expected to strain relations with adjoining landowners, or any other activities which to the ordinary person would be considered objectionable, offensive, or to cause embarrassment to Lessor or be detrimental to the Lessor's interest. Failure of Lessee to expel or deny access to the premises to any person or persons after being notified to do so by Lessor may result in the termination of this lease at discretion of Lessor.

## 14.

Modifications of this lease or special provisions shall be made in writing and signed copies of same will be attached to the original lease.

Thus done and signed on this _____ day of _____, 19____, in the presence of the undersigned witnesses.

WITNESSES:                     LESSOR

_____        _____

_____        _____


WITNESSES:                     LESSEE

_____        _____

_____

# 24

# From Field to Table—
# How to Have Tasty Venison

If you have ever heard someone refer to their "rank-flavored" venison, they were probably more to blame than the age of the animal or its type of feed.

By following some basic rules, you can set the table with venison that will rival the very best beef.

Unexcited animals make the best table fare. Quietly hunt your deer and take him with one well-placed shot in the vitals. You then have an animal that died with a normal heart rate and adrenaline flow—this makes for good meat. Deer that have been chased or wounded for long periods will usually have an "off," or rank, flavor. This undesirable taste results from the excessive by-products of exertion and fatigue that are deposited in muscle tissue.

## Field Dressing

Proper field dressing is a must. Immediately remove all the intestines and internal organs. Don't leave the chest cavity full of lungs, heart, etc. Wipe out the body cavity thoroughly with a dry cloth or dry, clean leaves.

Rapid and thorough cooling is necessary to insure quality meat. The carcass will cool faster if you spread the ribs apart with a stick, allowing the body heat to escape the cavity. If you plan to leave the deer in the field overnight, it must be cooled immedi-

*Proper field care of your deer can maintain the value of the venison.*

ately. If you have only a short distance to camp or home, the animal can be safely transported before cooling.

Be sure to drain off all excess blood in the body cavity and trim away any parts damaged by gunshot. If you plan to leave the animal in the field for a day or more, skin and wash it clean of any dirt or hair. Then, place the carcass in a sack or wrap it in a porous cloth to cool. The covering should be porous enough to allow air circulation, but tightly woven to give good protection from insects. The carcass can be hung by using a small block and tackle, or just by looping a rope over a tree limb.

A common practice is to place a stout stick through the gambrels of the hind legs, tie a rope to the center of the stick, hoist the deer off the ground, and then tie the rope securely to a nearby tree.

But sometimes it is advantageous to hang the deer by its antlers. If you want to mount your trophy, this will keep blood from getting into the neck and head. Also, a deer's hair angles toward the rump. By hanging the carcass by the head, the hairs will shed rain and snow, and the chest cavity will not collect blood or moisture. The proper way to hang a deer is an ongoing controversy, so try it both ways to see if your venison is best hanging head up or down.

Hang the meat in the shade where there is good circulation. Adequate cooling may take several hours. Sprinkle black pepper on the raw edges of the carcass and exposed meat to keep flies away.

Keep the carcass as cool and clean as possible on the trip home. Never lay it on a hot fender or hood.

Unpack the meat as soon as you arrive home. After skinning the deer, wash it with clear, cold water—use a brush if necessary to remove dirt, leaves, blood, and hair. Let the carcass drip dry. By doing so, a protective glaze will form that helps to keep the carcass free from contamination.

Age the carcass in a cool, dry place. Meat that is hung in a near-constant temperature, preferably 34 to 36 degrees F, will be more flavorful and tender. Proper aging also gives the meat a firmer "set," so the carcass can be cut and wrapped more easily. Walk-in coolers are best for aging, because they maintain a constant temperature and are free of odors and moisture. Off-odors are quickly transferred to meat and excess moisture will increase the development of mold. Allow the animal to age for at least two days before butchering.

How venison is cooked has a lot to do with whether or not you like it. The most common mistake is overcooking. Many cooks believe that because venison comes from a wild animal, it must be well done to kill impurities. Nothing could be further from the truth. Venison is probably one of the purest meats you will eat. It is free of chemicals and preservatives found in most of our food. It should never be cooked well done. Because of the minute amount of fat within the muscles, venison is quite dry. It should be cooked on low heat and served rare to medium to preserve its juiciness.

## Recipes

Here are some venison recipes that I have collected at various deer camps. They have been tested on scores of hungry hunters returning to the camp kitchen after a day in the swamps or hills trying to outwit whitetails.

## CEDAR CREEK LODGE MEAT LOAF

2 lbs. ground venison
½ lb. pork or sausage
1 tsp. salt & dash pepper
1 minced onion (up to ½ cup)
1 beaten egg

¼ cup chopped celery
1 cup soft bread crumbs
¼ cup chopped parsley
1 cup milk (1 cup tomatoes
    may be used instead)

Combine all ingredients and mold into a loaf. Line pan with foil and cook meat loaf uncovered for 2 hours in 350°F oven, or until done. Serves 8 to 10.

## VENISON MEATBALL APPETIZER

1 lb. ground venison
¼ cup milk
1 medium onion, minced
¾ tsp. salt
½ cup soft bread crumbs
1 cup flour

3 tbsp. butter
3 tbsp. prepared mustard
¼ tsp. thyme
3 tbsp. each molasses and
    vinegar
¼ cup ketchup

Combine first five ingredients, shape into bite-sized meatballs and flower lightly. In skillet, melt butter and brown meatballs. Remove meatballs, combine remaining ingredients and stir into skillet. Bring to a boil, add meatballs, and simmer 10 minutes, stirring occasionally. Yield: 50 meatballs.

## SWEET AND SOUR VENISON

2 lbs. cubed venison
½ tsp. salt, dash pepper
1 beaten egg
2 tbsp. flour
1 crushed garlic clove
½ cup salad oil
1 cup chicken bouillon

3 large green peppers
1 can (8 oz.) pineapple chunks
½ cup sugar
2½ tbsp. cornstarch
½ cup vinegar
2 tsp. soy sauce
cooked rice

Chop and boil peppers about 3 minutes, drain and set aside. Batter venison chunks in mixture of flour, egg, salt, and pepper. Brown in oil and garlic in frypan. Remove venison and retain 1 tbsp. of cooking oil in pan. Return venison to pan and add ⅓ cup of chicken bouillon; simmer for 10 minutes. Add pineapple and peppers. Combine sugar, cornstarch, vinegar, and soy sauce with remaining bouillon and add to frypan. Cook, stirring constantly until mixture is thick and hot. Serve over rice. Yield: 6 servings.

## BACKCOUNTRY VENISON STEW

| | |
|---|---|
| 2 lbs. venison cut in 1-in. cubes | ¾ cup chopped onion |
| 4 tbsp. bacon drippings | 4 medium potatoes, cubed |
| Water | 6 medium carrots, sliced |
| 1 tsp. garlic salt | 1 green pepper, chopped |
| 1 tsp. Worcestershire sauce | 2 cups sliced celery |
| 1½ tsp. salt | 3 tbsp. all-purpose flour |
| ½ tsp. black pepper | ¼ cup cold water |

Brown venison cubes in hot bacon drippings in heavy Dutch oven. Add water to cover, seasonings, and onion. Cover and simmer about 2 hours. Add potatoes, carrots, pepper, and celery, and cook about 20 minutes or until vegetables are tender. Taste and add more seasonings if desired. Dissolve flour in ¼ cup cold water and stir into stew. Cook about 5 minutes and serve hot. Yield: 8 servings.

## STAGSHEAD LODGE ROAST VENISON

| | |
|---|---|
| 1 8–10 lb. venison roast | Approx. ½ cup warm water |
| Salt & pepper to taste | Worcestershire sauce |
| 1 apple, peeled and sliced | Commercial barbecue sauce |
| 1 (1⅜ oz. pkg.) dry onion soup mix | (optional) |

Trim all fat from roast. Salt and pepper meat and place in roasting pan. Cover top of roast with apple slices. Stir onion soup mix into just enough warm water (about ½ cup) to make a paste; spread over roast and layers of apples. Sprinkle with Worcestershire sauce. Add ½ cup water to roasting pan. Cover and cook at 250°F for 6–7 hours. Add water as needed to keep roast from sticking. Test for doneness.

Discard pan liquid and apples before serving. Serve as entree with barbecue sauce, if desired. May also be served as an appetizer; cut venison into small pieces, insert toothpicks, and dip into barbecue sauce. Yield: 14 to 18 servings. This is an excellent recipe for older, tougher bucks.

## VENISON SPANISH RICE

2 slices bacon, chopped
½ lb. ground venison
½ cup chopped onion
Steamed rice to serve 4
1 #303 can stewed tomatoes
   (with celery, green pepper,
   and onion)

½ tsp. salt
⅛ tsp. pepper
⅛ tsp. paprika
½ tsp. chili powder

Saute bacon pieces, add onion and venison, breaking meat into small pieces. Add seasonings and cook until almost done. Add tomatoes and simmer 20–30 minutes longer. Serve over steamed rice. Yield: 4 servings.

## VENISON TERIYAKI

2 lbs. sirloin or round steak,
   1½ to 2 inches thick
1 can beef consomme
   (condensed)
1 clove garlic

¼ cup chopped onion
½ cup soy sauce
2 tbsp. lemon juice
1 tsp. seasoned salt
1 tbsp. brown sugar

Slice meat diagonally across the grain about ¼-inch thick. Prepare marinade by combining remaining ingredients. Pour the marinade over the meat and refrigerate overnight.

Drain meat and broil 3–4 inches from heat about 5 minutes. Baste with marinade, broil other side. Simmer remaining marinade to serve hot with meat. Makes 6 servings.

## VENISON SWISS STEAK IN SOUR CREAM

2 lbs. sirloin or round steak,
   1 inch thick
¼ cup bacon fat or other fat
1 clove garlic, crushed
¼ cup onions, minced
2 cups water
1 bay leaf

1 cup tart fruit juice,
   cranberry or apple
8 peppercorns
1 tsp. salt
1 tbsp. butter
4 tbsp. flour
¾ cup sour cream

Cut venison into 2-inch pieces. Melt fat in heavy skillet. Add meat and garlic, and saute until brown on all sides. Arrange meat in 2-quart casserole.

Put onions in skillet and cook 2 minutes in remaining fat. Add water, juices, bay leaf, peppercorns and salt. Pour this mixture over venison in casserole.

Bake in slow oven 325°F for 30–60 minutes (or until meat is tender). Melt butter in frypan, stir in flour. Stir constantly until smooth. Add cream and cook at low temperature for five minutes. Pour over meat in casserole. Serve immediately with buttered noodles or plain.

## VENISON SOUP

*1 lb. venison cut into bite-size pieces*
*1 large can stewed tomatoes*
*Worcestershire sauce to taste*
*3 medium carrots, sliced*
*3-4 small summer squash, cut up*
*4 large potatoes, cubed*
*1-46 oz. can V-8 juice*
*Tabasco sauce to taste*
*2 large onions, cut up*
*3-4 celery stalks, sliced*
*2 bell peppers, cut up*

Put all ingredients into large covered Dutch oven or large covered pot. Bring to a low boil and cook until vegetables are tender over low heat. NOTE: Vegetables can be interchanged with whatever is desired. Quantity of vegetables in soup depends on size of vegetable used.

*Venison soup includes tomatoes, carrots, potatoes, celery, and summer squash.*

## BRAISED VENISON CHOPS

*4 tbsp. cooking oil*  
*2 lbs. venison chops*  
*¼ cup onion flakes*  
*1¼ tsp. salt*  

*¼ cup Tabasco sauce*  
*½ cup beer or ale*  
*3 tbsp. biscuit mix*  
*½ cup currant jelly (optional)*  

Heat oil in heavy skillet or Dutch oven. Brown chops evenly. Add onions, sprinkle with salt and Tabasco. Add beer. Cover and cook over low heat about 15 minutes or until meat is tender. Remove chops to platter and keep hot. Combine biscuit mix and currant jelly. Stir into sauce in skillet. Cook over low heat, stirring until sauce thickens slightly. Pour over chops. Serve immediately.

## VENISON CHILI

This recipe is best when made a day ahead of time as the flavors have a chance to blend well.

*3 tbsp. salad oil*  
*1 large onion, chopped*  
*2 cloves garlic, chopped*  
*2 lbs. ground venison*  
*1-4 oz. can green chilies*  
*1-10 oz. can beef consomme*  

*1-6 oz. can tomato paste*  
*1-14½ oz. can stewed tomatoes*  
*1 tsp. oregano*  
*2 tsp. ground cumin*  
*1 to 3 tsp. chili powder*  
*2 cans kidney beans*  

In Dutch oven or large covered skillet, saute onion and garlic in oil until golden but not brown. Add crumbled venison and cook, stirring often until mixture is browned. Stir in chilies with their juice, consomme, tomato paste, tomatoes, chili powder, oregano, cumin, and bring to boiling point. Cover and simmer for 30 minutes. Add beans with their juice and stir to blend flavors. Add more chili powder if desired and simmer for an additional 10 minutes. Remove from heat, let chili cool, then cover and refrigerate until serving. Before heating and serving, skim any excess fat from top of chili and heat at low temperature to prevent burning.

May be garnished with shredded Monterey Jack or cheddar cheese, and green pepper or onion rings.

## VENISON JERKY

Every summer I find a few cuts of venison left in my freezer, usually roasts and round steaks. I have found that it is a simple process to convert these leftovers into tasty jerky in my own kitchen. In one Saturday afternoon, with visions of the forthcoming deer season, you can prepare enough jerky to supply noon snacks for the entire deer season. (This method works just as well with lean beef.)

*Step 1:* Trim off all fat and cut the meat along the grain into six-inch strips about one-half inch thick. Do not cut across the grain.

*Step 2:* Season the strips with salt, pepper, and liquid smoke or seasoning salt.

*Step 3:* Stick a round toothpick through one end of each strip.

*Step 4:* Suspend the strips from the oven rack, turning the heat on to 120 degrees. Leave the oven door slightly open so the moisture can escape. Heat the strips for about five hours or until the meat has turned black and there is no moisture in the center. When the strips are done, they should be completely dry, but flexible enough to bend without breaking.

Jerky has a high nutritional value and will keep for months without refrigeration. In fact, the only problem I have had with my kitchen jerky is keeping my family from eating all of it while we're planning our fall trips.

With a little care, venison can be tasty. Follow the rules from field to table, and enjoy your deer for many meals.

# 25

# How to Tan a Deer Hide

E ach year, untold thousands of deer hides are discarded because hunters don't know how to tan the skin or because
custom tanning is too expensive. Any hunter who is willing to
put forth some effort can tan deer hides right at home.

A deerskin tanned with the hair still on it makes a handsome
wall-hanging or table cover. Skin tanned without the hair, called
*buckskin,* can be used to make gun cases, gloves, moccasins,
shirts, and many other items.

One reason that home tanning has never become popular is
that it does take time and involves some hard work. The skill of
home tanning is easy to learn, but it will take a few skins before
you master it. When possible, it's advisable to tan a few practice
skins before you tackle a trophy hide.

The information in this chapter will show you how to turn
that deer skin into something useful. With some practice and patience, you can beat the high cost of leather by making your own.
For those who can say "I tanned it myself," there is a great deal
of pride and satisfaction.

**Step 1**

The first and most important step in deerskin tanning is to
remove all of the flesh, fat and membranous tissue. This can best
be done by laying the skin, flesh side up, on a flat surface or on a

***Step 1***

fleshing beam. I use a portable work table with a 2x6-inch board secured in it on a 45-degree angle. Using a sharp knife, remove every trace of flesh. This is a slow, time-consuming job, but necessary for good tanning. The skin will not tan where there is any flesh, fat, or tough membrane. If you plan to tan a skin with hair on it, skip steps 2 and 3 and proceed with step 4.

*Step 2*

## Step 2

If the skin is to be made into buckskin, it's necessary to re-move the hair. This can be done by mixing the following in a large plastic garbage can: one gallon of hardwood ashes, two pounds of household (slaked) lime, and five gallons of warm wa-ter. Stir these ingredients with a stick until dissolved. Put in the deer skin and make sure it is completely immersed. Stir the skin with the stick three or four times a day until the hair comes off easily. This will usually take two or three days. Don't leave the skin in this mixture any longer than necessary.

## Step 3

Remove the skin from the ashes/lime mixture and rinse with water. Place on a flat surface or fleshing board, hair side up, and rub off the hair with the back of a knife blade. Rinse the de-haired skin several times in clean water and soak 24 hours in a

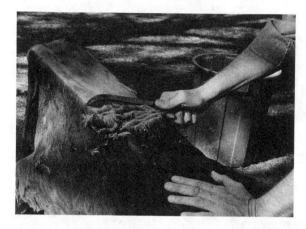

***Step 3***

garbage can in a mixture of ten gallons of water to two quarts of vinegar. Stir every few hours. At the end of the soaking time, empty the garbage can and refill it with clean water. Soak the skin overnight. At this point, it is always advisable to once again check the skin, making sure that all hair, flesh, fat, and membrane have been removed. The skin is now ready for tanning.

***Step 4***

## Step 4

In a small plastic bucket, dissolve one pound of alum in one gallon of warm water. In the large garbage can, dissolve two and a half pounds of salt in four gallons of water. Pour the alum solution into the garbage can with the salt solution. Stir, mixing the two thoroughly. Place the skin in this solution and soak from six to eight days. Stir the solution during the soaking period at least twice a day to make sure that all parts of the skin are reached. After the soaking period, remove the skin, drain it thoroughly, and rinse for at least 20 minutes in running water.

*Step 5*

## Step 5

Tack the wet skin to a flat surface such as a sheet of plywood. If you are tanning a skin with the hair on, tack the skin with the flesh side out. Allow it to partially dry, being sure to keep it out of the sun. When it is almost dry, rub the skin with a light coating of warm neat's-foot oil. Remove the skin from the flat surface and rub the other side with the warm oil. Wipe off excess oil with a cloth. Now the real work of the tanning process begins.

*Step 6*

## Step 6

The success or failure of most tanned skins depends on this step. Keep the skin damp, but not wet, with a well-moistened cloth. Rub the skin back and forth over a dull edge until the skin is supple and soft. The edge of a fleshing board, carpenter's sawhorse, or dull ax head clamped in a vise will work. As the softening progresses, *lightly* rub some warm neat's-foot oil on the skin. Don't overdo it or you will wind up with an oily mess. Work every inch of the skin over the dull edge until it is as soft as a chamois cloth. Be sure to keep the skin damp and keep working it until soft. This will take some time; it's a lot more work than most people think. Obviously, if you are working with a skin that has the hair on it, work only the flesh side.

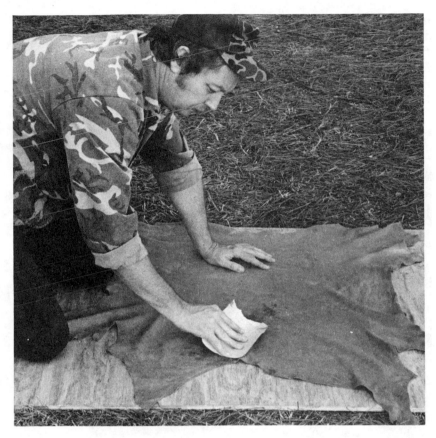

**Step 7**

## Step 7

Once the skin is soft and pliable, it is time to "finish" it. Lay the tanned hide on a flat surface. Rub fine sandpaper over every inch to smooth the surface. Only do the flesh side if you have tanned a skin with hair on it. When the skin takes on a smooth appearance it is ready to be used as a rug, or to be cut and sewed into some other useful item.

A home-tanned rug or buckskin is something to cherish, as it reflects a lot of work and the knowledge of a pioneer skill. Clothes made from home-tanned skins are durable and are a must for a muzzleloading-rifle shooter. Most beginning tanners are surprised by the number of skins it takes to make garments. Depending upon the size of the deer skins, it may take three or four to make a shirt, and nine or ten to make a complete mountainman outfit. But in the end, you can proudly say you did the whole thing yourself.

**Fears wears a home-made buckskin outfit.**

# 26

# Be a Safe, Ethical Hunter

I t was difficult to decide whether this chapter would be at the beginning or end of this book. The information is so important that it should be the first thing hunters read. But it should also be the last thing they read, so it remains fresh on their minds on their next trip afield.

Having spent my entire adult life as a professional wildlife manager and hunting guide, I have seen the sadness and suffering that come from hunting accidents. I have also seen the amount of work and stress that goes into search and rescue operations for hunters who were unprepared to go afield. For these and many other reasons, every hunter should be required to pass a hunter safety course.

I also believe that every deer hunter should take a basic survival course and complete a session in Red Cross First Aid and CPR training. Some states are now offering advanced hunter education courses with heavy emphasis on ethical considerations, wildlife behavior, and many other facets of hunting. Such courses can go a long way toward making you a better hunter, one who has a greater respect for wildlife, the outdoors, and private landowners.

If every hunter had these different types of training, many accidents and rescue operations would never occur. Whether you shoot a muzzleloader, a bow, or a modern firearm, it is your responsibility to follow some basic rules of safety. These rules apply whenever and wherever firearms are being handled. Here, according to the National Rifle Association, are rules that hunters should practice at all times:

1.   Always keep a gun's muzzle pointed in a safe direction.

2.   Treat every firearm as if it were loaded, even when you think it is not.

3.   Keep the action of the firearm open, except when actually shooting or when storing an unloaded gun.

4.   Use the right ammunition for your firearm. Carry only one type of ammunition to be sure you will not mix different types.

5.   Be sure of your target and beyond. Identify the target, then look past it to make sure it is safe to shoot. Do not shoot where your bullets might ricochet off rocks, trees, metal, water, or other hard surfaces.

6.   Alcohol, drugs, and shooting do not mix. Drugs and alcohol may impair your judgment. Keen judgment is essential to safe shooting.

7.   Beware of fatigue. When you become so tired that hunting isn't fun any more, go back to camp. Fatigue can cause carelessness and clumsiness, which can cause accidents. Fatigue can make you see things that aren't really there.

8.   When you have finished hunting, unload your gun before returning it to your vehicle or camp. When you arrive home, double-check the gun before you store it.

Most of these same rules apply to the bowhunter. Also, the bowhunter has another responsibility—to keep his broadhead covered at all times except when the arrow is actually nocked. Always be aware of where people are around you when you have a broadhead exposed.

When you are traveling with a firearm, whether by automobile, boat, horse, motorcycle or plane, be sure that the gun is always unloaded. Place it in a protective case, if possible. Position the firearm securely, so it will not move about during travel. To transport a gun on a public means of transportation, such as a bus, train, or plane, check first with the carrier's agent concerning their regulations.

Another word of caution is unload your gun before climbing a steep bank, traveling across slippery ground, or crossing a stream or fence. When you are alone and must cross a fence, unload your firearm, and place it under the fence with the muzzle

*Always unload your firearm before placing it back in the vehicle.*

pointed away from where you are crossing. When hunting with others, unload the gun and keep the action open. Have one of your companions hold the gun while you cross. Once over the fence, take the gun and your companion's unloaded gun so he can cross safely.

Many accidents occur each year by hunters using tree stands, both permanent and portable. Keep these safety measures in mind:

1. Be sure your portable platform is securely chained or strapped in the tree. Check the platform itself for loose bolts or screws each time you use it.

2. Never attempt to use a permanent stand that you are unsure of; it may be rickety or contain rotten wood that will collapse under your weight.

3. Never sit or stand in a tree stand without some kind of safety belt attached to the tree.

4. Don't tie yourself in with a rope. The rope will draw tight around your chest and leave you dangling. If you fall, fling your firearm or bow and broadheads as far away as possible.

5. Since you will likely be climbing up the tree before daylight and down after dark, practice with any portable tree stand at home before attempting to use it in the woods.

6. Never climb with a firearm, or bow and sharp broadheads (even in a bow quiver) in your hand. Raise and lower them with a rope.

7. Be sure that any firearm is unloaded and the action open when raising and lowering it to and from the stand.

At home, always assume that anyone untrained in the use of a firearm will not know how to handle it properly. To prevent accidents, always store firearms and ammunition separately in locked storage units.

Remember that firearms are precision instruments. If your gun is not working properly, do not hunt with it or take it shooting. Have the gun examined by a competent gunsmith or return it to the manufacturer. Even minor repairs should be made by an expert. Beginning and inexperienced shooters should never attempt to repair any firearms.

All hunters should let someone know when and where they are going and when they expect to return. Doing this is your insurance that help will be on the way soon.

Hunters should also understand such things as hypothermia and how to treat the condition. If you are going on a guided hunt, be sure to let your guides know beforehand if you have any special health problems. Do the same with your hunting companions. Then, if you get into any kind of problem, they will know what action to take.

Hunting is usually fun and relaxing—we do not anticipate a life-threatening situation. But many hunters suddenly find themselves in dangerous predicaments. One way to avoid many problems is to get into excellent physical condition prior to the hunting season. Your stamina and muscle tone have a lot to do with how well you hunt and how much enjoyment you derive from it. Know your limitations and stay within them. I have seen many hunters pay several thousand dollars for once-in-a-lifetime hunts for big game, only to end up sitting around camp after the first few days, suffering from blisters, strained muscles, or sprained ankles.

**Hunting Ethics**

If the sport of hunting is to survive, every hunter must become more ethical while afield. Whether hunting with companions or alone deep in the backcountry, a conscientious hunter follows a code of ethics. Here are some rules which should be a part of your hunting code of ethics.

**Ethical hunters make every effort to trail and find wounded game.**

1.   I will consider myself an invited guest of the landowner, seeking his permission, and conducting myself so I will be welcome in the future.

2.   I will obey the rules of safe gun handling and will courteously, but firmly insist that others do the same.

3.   I will obey all game laws and regulations, and will insist that my companions do likewise.

4.   I will do my best to acquire those marksmanship and hunting skills that assure clean, sportsmanlike kills.

5.   I will support conservation efforts that can assure good hunting for future generations of Americans.

6.   I will pass along to younger hunters the attitudes and skills essential to a true outdoorsman.

7.   I will treat the game that I am hunting with respect. I realize it is my responsibility to retrieve all downed game, regardless of the amount of time it takes.

8.   I will use all game taken for food purposes and make sure that none is wasted in any way.

9.   I realize that the success of a hunting trip is not measured by how quickly I can take my limit or if I take any game at all. I will strive to enjoy the hunt as a means of recreation, of which the taking of game is only a small part.

If every sportsman pledges to be an ethical hunter, we will have many, many more places to hunt. Ethics have become a vital part of our sport—it behooves us to re-pledge ourselves to following these important rules.

*Hunting provides enjoyable recreation for millions of Americans. Whether future generations will be able to enjoy the sport depends in large part on the actions of today's hunters.*

# Index